MORE ANSWERS THAN QUESTIONS

MORE ANSWERS THAN QUESTIONS

WHERE EVERY QUIZ HAS MANY ANSWERS

AND YOU NEED TO FIND THEM ALL!

DANIEL SMITH

Michael O'Mara Books Limited

For Mum and Dad – all those Christmases playing Trivial Pursuit have come to this!

First published in Great Britain in 2018 by
Michael O'Mara Books Limited
9 Lion Yard
Tremadoc Road
London SW4 7NQ

A CIP catalogue record for this book is available from the British Library.

Papers used by Michael O'Mara Books Limited are natural, recyclable products made from wood grown in sustainable forests. The manufacturing processes conform to the environmental regulations of the country of origin.

ISBN: 978-1-78243-913-4 in paperback print format
ISBN: 978-1-78243-930-1 in ebook format

1 3 5 7 9 10 8 6 4 2

Co…
De…

Pri… by CPI Group (UK) Ltd, Croydon, CR0 4YY

Fo…

www.mombooks.com

Introduction

This is a quiz book with a difference. The further you get into each quiz, the more answers each question asks for. By the time you get to the last question of each quiz (the mystery question eleven), you might need to come up with literally dozens of answers!

So how does it work? Like lots of quiz books, this one will challenge the breadth of your knowledge. The subjects covered range from science and space to geography, food, sport and the arts – and pretty much everything in between. But *More Answers Than Questions* is designed to also probe the depth of your knowledge. Just how much do you really know about any given subject? Here is your chance not only to prove just how clever you are, but also to fill in some of the gaps in your knowledge – perhaps even gaps you did not know you had.

I can guarantee that no one will know all the answers to these quizzes. In fact, if anyone did, their abilities would be such that they really ought to be using their time doing something incredible to improve the future of the human race rather than idling their time immersed in trivia. By the same token, most people will be able to get a good few of the answers. So if you're not a solo quiz fiend who wants to take on the full scope of the 700-plus questions and the several thousand answers contained within (and it is a task that some eager quiz addicts will lap up), it's a good idea to get a gang of friends and family together to tackle the challenge as one. Where some quizzes can reduce a convivial atmosphere to a climate of rancorous competitiveness within minutes, the posers contained within positively encourage a collegiate effort. Everyone can have their chance to shine as you work as a team to master each set of questions.

So get on your thinking caps, pull up a comfy chair and prepare to be thoroughly tested. Bathe in the glory of getting some things right, embrace the frustration of chasing some elusive fact or other from the darkest recesses of your mind, and delight at learning a host of weird and wonderful facts that you'll probably never need to dredge up again!

Questions

General Knowledge I

1

From which flower do you get vanilla pods?

2

What are the names of the two brothers who featured in the rock band Oasis?

3

What are Germany's three largest cities by population?

4

The heads of which four US presidents are carved into Mount Rushmore?

5

Who were the original five members of the 'Rat Pack'?

6

The classic Rubik's cube was decorated with which six colours?

7

What were the Seven Wonders of the Ancient World?

8

As of 2016, eight men had won eight or more gold medals at Olympic Summer Games. Can you name them all?

9

There are nine capital cities that begin with the letter 'D'. What are they?

10

The Mississippi River runs through or along which ten US states?

11

Can you explain what each of the following professions does or did? Apothecary, brazier, chandler, chiffonnier, cooper, costermonger, hostler, scrivener, stevedore, tanner and wainwright.

Answers on page 140

Countries of the World

1

Which country lies entirely within South Africa?

2

New Zealand has two overseas states. What are they?

3

What are the three 'Benelux' countries?

4

There are four sovereign nations beginning with the letter 'D'. What are they?

5

What are the modern names of the countries known previously as Abyssinia, British Honduras, Ceylon, Siam and Southern Rhodesia?

6

Which six countries have the world's largest known oil reserves?

7

Hungary is bordered by which seven nations?

8

Which eight territories and states make up Australia?

9

To which sovereign nations do the following territories belong? Åland Islands, Ashmore and Cartier Islands, Bouvet Island, Curaçao, Faroe Islands, Guam, Macao, Niue, and Saint Pierre and Miquelon.

10

Which ten countries boast the most UNESCO World Heritage Sites?

11

Fifteen states emerged out of the break-up of the Soviet Union in 1991. Can you name them all?

Answers on page 141

Sport I

1

As of 2018, which American football team had won the most Super Bowls?

2

Which two boxers contested the 'Rumble in the Jungle'?

3

Which three events make up a standard triathlon?

4

Golf's majors comprise which four tournaments?

5

Up to the 2015 tournament, which five countries have contested rugby union's World Cup final?

6

Which were the first six teams to win the UEFA Champions League that began in the 1992–93 season?

7

What are the seven positions in netball?

8

Up to 2014, which eight nations have won the soccer World Cup?

9

What are the nine fielding positions in baseball?

10

Which ten male tennis players have been ranked world number one for the longest time?

11

As of 2018, which twelve nations have hosted the Winter Olympic Games?

Answers on page 142

Cinema I

1

In which city is Bollywood based?

2

Which two characters had a 'Bogus Journey' in 1991?

3

What were the three colours of Krzysztof Kieślowski's 1990s film trilogy?

4

Who directed the following four films? *Amélie*, *Cinema Paradiso*, *Crouching Tiger, Hidden Dragon* and *Life Is Beautiful*.

5

What were the stage names of the five Marx Brothers?

6

To 2018, which six actors have depicted James Bond on screen?

7

What were the names of the seven dwarves in Walt Disney's 1937 movie, *Snow White and the Seven Dwarfs*?

8

Who played each of the following landmark film characters? Atticus Finch in *To Kill a Mockingbird*, Don Vito Corleone in *The Godfather*, Jack Sparrow in *Pirates of the Caribbean*, the Joker in *The Dark Knight*, Luke Skywalker in *Star Wars*, Norman Bates in *Psycho*, Rocky Balboa in *Rocky* and Tyler Durden in *Fight Club*.

9

Between 1968 and 2017, nine *Planet of the Apes* films have been made. Can you name them all?

10

In which screen musicals did the following songs appear? 'All That Jazz', 'Circle of Life', 'Don't Rain on My Parade', 'Edelweiss', 'Good Morning', 'Hopelessly Devoted to You', 'Let's Go Fly a Kite', 'The Boy Next Door', 'Time Warp' and 'Tomorrow Belongs to Me'.

11

There have been twelve Muppet films altogether up to 2018, but can you name them all?

Answers on page 143

Kings, Queens and Other Leaders

1

Who was the first Roman Emperor?

2

Kim Il-sung was the first leader of North Korea, but what are the names of the son and grandson who succeeded him?

3

Napoleon famously lived on which three islands?

4

Since the end of the Shogun era in 1867, Japan has had four emperors. What are their personal names?

5

Can you identify the ruler by their description? Queen of the United Kingdom from 1837–1901; Emperor of Ethiopia from 1930–74; King of France from 1774–92; King of Macedonia from 336–323 BC; Emperor of Russia from 1894–1917.

6

Who were the First Ladies to the following US presidents: George Washington, Franklin D. Roosevelt, John F. Kennedy, Richard Nixon, Gerald Ford and George Bush Snr?

7

Since William Henry Harrison passed away in 1841, a further seven US presidents have died in office. Who?

8

As of 2017, there had been eight permanent Secretaries-General of the United Nations. Can you name them?

9

Can you name the nine men who led the Soviet Union between 1922 and 1991, either as Chairman of the Council of People's Commissars, General (or First) Secretary of the Central Committee of the Communist Party or President of the Soviet Union.

10

From which royal houses/dynasties did the following monarchs hail: Cleopatra VII of Egypt, King Edward VII of the United Kingdom, Charles V of the Holy Roman Empire, Nicholas II of Russia, Elizabeth I of England, Charlemagne, Louis XIV of France, King Solomon, Victor Emmanuel II of Italy, and Puyi.

11

Can you name the fourteen people who have served as vice president of the United States between 1949 and 2018?

Answers on page 145

Land Animals

1

A cow's stomach is divided into how many distinct departments?

2

What is the name for the camel species with one hump and those with two?

3

What are the three fastest land mammals?

4

Can you identify the four heaviest land animals?

5

What are the traditional five Great Apes?

6

What are the six largest species of cat?

7

What do we call the male of the following species? Deer, donkey, goat, horse, swan, duck and sheep.

8

What are the eight main species classifications of bear?

9

What do we call the female of the following species? Alligator, deer, donkey, ferret, fox, goat, swan, sheep and zebra.

10

What do we call the offspring of the following ten animals? Deer, dragonfly, eel, goat, goose, hare, kangaroo, oyster, spider and swan.

11

Can you identify the animals from their scientific names? *Pongo, Bos Taurus, Canis lupus familiaris, Capra aegagrus hircus, Equus quagga, Loxodonta africana, Macropus rufus, Ovis aries, Pan troglodytes, Panthera leo, Sus scrofa domesticus and Vulpes vulpes.*

Answers on page 146

Literature I

1

Which Franz Kafka novel sees Gregor Samsa turn into a giant insect?

2

Which literary pairing made their debut in the story *A Study in Scarlet*?

3

What are the names of Fyodor Dostoyevsky's *Brothers Karamazov*?

4

What are the first four books of the Bible?

5

From which countries do or did the following authors hail? Jo Nesbø, Nikolai Gogol, Orhan Pamuk, André Brink and Milan Kundera.

6

The Lion, the Witch and the Wardrobe was the first of C. S. Lewis's *Chronicles of Narnia* to be published. What were the other six?

7

What are the seven books that make up the Harry Potter series?

8

What are the eight basic parts of speech in the Indo-European family of languages?

9

Who were the nine members of the Fellowship of the Ring?

10

Can you identify the Nobel Prize for Literature winners from their works? *The Beggar Maid, Being and Nothingness, The Bluest Eye, Buddenbrooks, The Good Terrorist, Just So Stories, One Day in the Life of Ivan Denisovich, Quo Vadis, Red Sorghum Clan* and *A Tale of Two Gardens.*

11

Can you name all 36 plays included in William Shakespeare's *First Folio*?

Answers on page 147

The 1940s

1

Which city hosted the 1948 Summer Olympic Games?

2

On which two Japanese cities did the USA drop atomic bombs in 1945?

3

Who were the 'big three' Allied leaders who met at the Yalta Conference as the Second World War neared its end in 1945?

4

Which four people constituted the classic line-up of The Ink Spots?

5

In which years did the following five events occur? D-Day, Japan attacks Pearl Harbor, Leon Trotsky is assassinated, NATO is established, the modern state of Israel is founded.

6

Who did the following six people marry (year of wedding in brackets)? Desi Arnaz (1940), Vivien Leigh (1940), Harry James (1943), Humphrey Bogart (1945), Philip Mountbatten (1947) and Prince Aly Khan (1949).

7

The first *Road to ...* movie, starring Bing Crosby, Bob Hope and Dorothy Lamour, came out in 1940. But can you remember the titles of all seven movies in the series?

8

Can you identify these eight notable people who died in the decade (initials, dates and professions provided)? N.T. (1856–1943, Serbian-American scientist and visionary); M.P. (1858–1947, German theoretical physicist); P.K. (1879–1940, Swiss-German artist); B.M. (1883–1945, Italian political leader); J.M.K. (1883–1946, British economist); S.E. (1898–1948, Soviet film-maker); L.G. (1903–41, American baseball star); C.L. (1908–42, American film actress).

9

Here are nine literary classics from the decade, but can you identify the author of each? *The Garden of Forking Paths*, *Common Sense Book of Baby and Child Care*, *The Diary of a Young Girl*, *The Gathering Storm*, *If This is a Man*, *Capitalism, Socialism and Democracy*, *Long Day's Journey Into Night*, *The Second Sex* and *The Stranger*.

10

Which ten films won the Best Picture Oscar between 1940 and 1949?

11

Which countries did the following figures lead during the 1940s? Aung San, Benito Mussolini, Charles de Gaulle, David Ben-Gurion, Francisco Franco, Fulgencio Batista, Getúlio Vargas, Ho Chi Minh, Liaquat Ali Khan, Peter Fraser, Reza Shah and Robert Menzies.

Answers on page 149

Games and Pastimes

1

What is the lowest score you cannot hit with one dart?

2

Which two chess players contested the world championship in a legendary match in Iceland in 1972?

3

What are the three most expensive properties on a classic US Monopoly board?

4

What are the four suits in a standard pack of cards?

5

Can you identify the martial arts from the following translations of their names: 'empty hand', 'the gentle way', 'the soft art', 'the way of harmonious spirit' and 'the way of the sword'?

6

Can you name the six standard chess pieces?

7

In Scrabble, which five letters are worth four points and which two letters are worth ten points?

8

What eight colours of ball are used in a game of snooker?

9

Aside from the cellar, can you name the nine rooms in the classic version of Cluedo?

10

Can you identify all ten poker hands?

11

Back to classic Cluedo, and can you name the six suspects and the six weapons?

Answers on page 150

Science I

1

What was the great discovery of James Watson, Francis Crick, Maurice Wilkins and Rosalind Franklin?

2

Pure water is composed of which two elements?

3

What are the three main classifications of rock?

4

The heart is made up of four chambers. What are they?

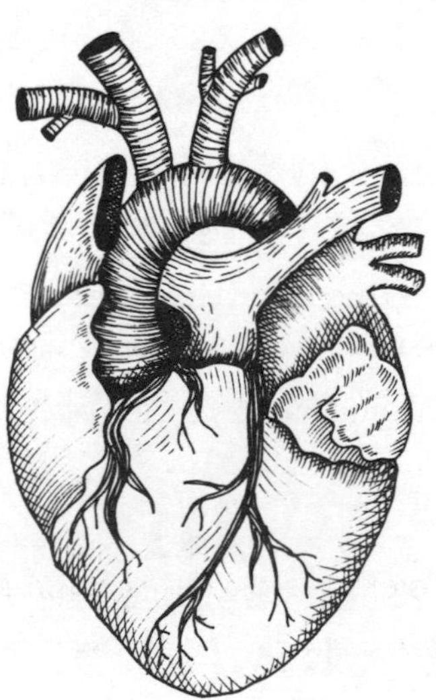

5

What are the five officially classified dwarf planets in our solar system?

6

What are the six alkali metals?

7

What are the seven base SI units?

8

Can you name the eight major standard taxonomic rankings?

9

Can you convert the following nine decimals into binary?
1, 2, 3, 4, 5, 10, 25, 50 and 100.

10

What do the following scales measure? Apgar, Beaufort, Douglas Sea, Fujita, Glasgow Coma, Kinsey, Mohs, pH, Richter and Scoville.

11

Which eleven elements are gases at room temperature?

Answers on page 151

Africa

1

Which former World Footballer of the Year became Liberia's president in 2018?

2

The Democratic Republic of Congo and the Republic of Congo are sometimes referred to by their respective capital cities, but what are they?

3

From which countries did Libya (1951), Burundi (1962) and Mozambique (1975) gain independence?

4

Using the International Organization for Standardization's two-letter coding system, which countries are represented by the codes TD, DZ, LY and ZA?

5

What are the traditional 'big five' African game animals?

6

What are the modern names of the countries known previously as Basutoland, Bechuanaland, Dahomey, the Gold Coast, Northern Rhodesia and Nyasaland?

7

The equator passes through which seven African nations?

8

Who wrote these classics of African literature? *Burger's Daughter*, *The Cairo Trilogy*, *Chaka*, *Disgrace*, *The Famished Road*, *Nervous Conditions*, *Arrow of God* and *Ake: The Years of Childhood*.

9

In which countries would you find these tourist attractions? Anse Intendance, Black River Gorges National Park, Djemaa el Fna, El Djem Amphitheatre, Fish River Canyon, Maasai Mara National Reserve, Okavango Delta, Pyramids of Giza and Table Mountain.

10

From which country did each of these national leaders come? Haile Selassie, Hastings Banda, Idi Amin, Jean-Bédel Bokassa, Jomo Kenyatta, Kenneth Kaunda, Kwame Nkrumah, Mobutu Sese Seko, Nelson Mandela and Omar Bongo.

11

Can you name the capital cities for each of these fifteen countries? Angola, Botswana, Burkina Faso, Egypt, Ethiopia, Kenya, Liberia, Madagascar, Morocco, Namibia, Nigeria, Rwanda, Sierra Leone, Sudan and Zambia.

Answers on page 153

Transport

1

In which decade did London's underground railway – the world's first – start operating?

2

What were the first names of the aviation pioneers the Wright brothers?

3

What are the nautical terms for the front of a sailing vessel, a measurement of depth equivalent to six feet and a unit of speed equivalent to one nautical mile per hour?

4

Which motor companies produced the Model T, Silver Ghost, Elan and Beetle models?

5

Can you identify these bridges from the clues? Suspension bridge straddling San Francisco Bay; half-completed bridge in former papal city of France; ancient, shop-lined bridge across the River Arno in Florence; bridge connecting Malmö in Sweden with Copenhagen in Denmark; cantilever bridge spanning the Hooghly river in Kolkata, India.

6

In which cities will you find the following railway stations? Atocha Station, Caminho de Ferro de Moçambique Railway Station, Chhatrapati Shivaji Terminus, Gare du Nord, Sirkeci Station and Waverley Station.

7

Starting with the earliest, which were the first seven countries to send satellites into orbit?

8

Can you identify the famous cars associated with these films and television series? *Back to the Future*, *Dukes of Hazzard*, *Goldfinger*, *Harry Potter and the Chamber of Secrets*, *Knightrider*, Lady Penelope's car in *Thunderbirds*, *Starsky and Hutch*, and *The A-Team*.

9

In which countries would you find these nine famous motor racing circuits? Mount Panorama Bathurst, Estoril, Hungaroring, Interlagos, Laguna Seca, Le Mans, Monza, Silverstone and Spa-Francorchamps.

10

Here are ten International Air Transport Association codes, but which airports do they denote? ARN, BAI, JFK, LAX, LHR, LOS, NRT, SHA, SYD and TXL.

11

In which countries did the following motor manufacturers originate? Dacia, Ford, Hyundai, Maserati, Renault, Saab, SAIC, SEAT, Škoda, Tata, Toyota and Volkswagen.

Answers on page 154

Music I

1

Who was the subject of Elton John's original recording of 'Candle in the Wind'?

2

Whose professional rivalry was examined in Miloš Forman's 1984 movie, *Amadeus*?

3

Can you name the Three Tenors?

4

Can you remember the four-man line-up of The Monkees?

5

The five Spice Girls went by which nicknames?

6

In the Western classical tradition, bass is the lowest traditional vocal type classification. What are the other six?

7

Michael Jackson's classic album *Thriller* produced seven singles that all reached the top ten in the US Billboard chart. Can you name them all?

8

By what nicknames were the following jazz musicians commonly known: Louis Armstrong, Edward Kennedy Ellington, William Basie, John Gillespie, Billie Holiday, Julian Adderley, Thomas Waller and Charlie Parker?

9

According to the popular song, what are the names of Father Christmas's nine reindeer (one of whom has a red nose)?

10

Can you name the composers of the following operas: *Don Giovanni* (1787), *Fidelio* (1805), *The Barber of Seville* (1816), *La Traviata* (1853), *Carmen* (1875), *Der Ring des Nibelungen* (1876), *Eugene Onegin* (1879), *Tosca* (1900), *Peter Grimes* (1945) and *Nixon in China* (1987)?

11

Can you identify the stars of popular music from their birth names: Paul Hewson, Reginald Dwight, Stevland Hardaway Judkins, David Jones, Farrokh Bulsara, Georgios Panayiotou, Gordon Sumner, Anna Mae Bullock, Robert Zimmerman, Brian Warner, Chaim Witz, James Newell Osterberg Jr, Michael Balzary, Marvin Aday, John Ritchie and Saul Hudson?

Answers on page 155

General Knowledge II

1

Greenland is an autonomous territory of which country?

2

What are the names of the two Atlantic archipelagos that have the status of autonomous regions of Portugal?

3

What are the three largest Abrahamic religions?

4

Can you name the four houses at the Hogwarts School of Witchcraft and Wizardry?

5

In *The Simpsons*, who are the five permanent members of the Simpsons' household?

6

What are the six major classifications of triangles?

7

Which seven nations are considered to make up Central America?

8

Can you name all eight members in the classic line-ups of the rock groups The Beatles and Queen?

9

Which nine countries border the Baltic Sea?

10

Besides Ireland and its variant name of Eire, ten other countries have four letters in their name. What are they?

11

What were the gifts presented in the song 'The Twelve Days of Christmas'?

Answers on page 156

History I

1

What was the name of the Portuguese explorer who was the first European to reach India by sea?

2

What were the official capitals of West and East Germany?

3

What were the names of the three ships Christopher Columbus took on his first voyage to the New World in 1492?

4

Which four US presidents have been assassinated?

5

Who were the five emperors of Rome's Julio-Claudian dynasty (27 BC–AD 68)?

6

Who were the six wives of England's King Henry VIII?

7

Can you identify the seven leaders from their nicknames? 'Dubya', 'Honest Abe', 'Ike', 'Mutti', 'The Iron Lady', 'The Little Corporal' and 'Tricky Dicky'.

8

Who achieved these eight famous firsts? Animal to orbit the earth; athlete to retain the Olympic 100m and 200m titles; female prime minister of Pakistan; to run a marathon (according to Greek legend); to run a mile in under four minutes; to sail single-handed and non-stop around the world; surgeon to carry out a human heart transplant; leader of first party to reach the South Pole.

9

Can you identify these nine famous battles from their dates and location? 31 BC, Acarnarnia; 1066, England; 1097 to 1098, Turkey; 1415, France; 1805, Moravia; 1863, Pennsylvania; 1917, Belgium; 1944, Italy; 1968, South Vietnam.

10

In which years did these events occur? Al Qaeda attack on the World Trade Centre; Christopher Columbus discovers the New World; dissolution of the USSR; end of the American Civil War; end of the First World War; Mao Zedong becomes China's leader; Nelson Mandela becomes South Africa's president; Partition of India; signing of Magna Carta; US Declaration of Independence.

11

After whom were these places named? Bolivia, Colombia, El Salvador, Georgetown (Guyana), Monrovia (Liberia), Pittsburgh (USA), Port Louis (Mauritius), Pretoria (South Africa), Athens (Greece), Sydney (Australia), Virginia (USA) and Washington, D.C (USA).

Answers on page 157

Geography I

1

In which country is Lake Balaton situated?

2

Which two cities were at the beginning and end of the original route of the Orient Express?

3

After Mount Everest, what are the three highest peaks in the Himalayas?

4

Which four countries begin with the letter 'V'?

5

What are the five most populous Caribbean sovereign nations?

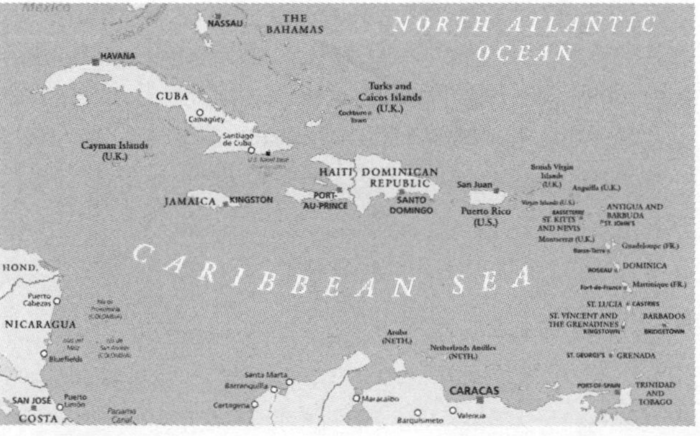

6

Can you name the longest river in each of Africa, Asia, North America, South America, Australasia and Europe?

7

According to the World Warterfall Database, what are the world's seven tallest waterfalls?

8

What are the world's eight largest lakes by area?

9

Where in the world will you find the following nine landmarks? Acropolis, CN Tower, the Colosseum, Hagia Sophia, Heroes' Square, the Kremlin, Valley of the Kings, Victoria Harbour and the World Archipelago.

10

Can you name the ten smallest sovereign countries in the world by area?

11

Which currencies do the following countries use? Brazil, China, Czech Republic, Hungary, Israel, Japan, Malaysia, Morocco, Poland, Russia, Venezuela and Vietnam.

Answers on page 159

The 1950s

1

Which US civil rights campaigner famously refused to give up her bus seat in 1955?

2

Which cities were the primary hosts of the Summer Olympic Games in 1952 and 1956?

3

What were the first names of the three Beverley Sisters?

4

In which year did the following events take place? James Dean is killed in a car accident; the Soviet satellite Sputnik is launched; the summit of Mount Everest is conquered for the first time; Winston Churchill begins his second term as British prime minister.

5

Can you identify these *Time* magazine Persons of the Year from the year and initials? 1953 (K.A.), 1954 (J.F.D), 1957 (N.K.), 1958 (C.D.G.) and 1959 (D.D.E.).

6

Who were the six original members of the European Economic Community created by the Treaty of Rome of 1957?

7

Who did the following seven people marry (year of wedding in brackets)? Anne Frances Robbins (1952), Roger Vadim (1952), Jacqueline Bouvier (1953), Mel Ferrer (1954), Arthur Miller (1956), Prince Rainier of Monaco (1956) and Robert Wagner (1957).

8

Identify these eight notable people who died in the decade (initials, dates and professions provided)? W.R.H. (1863–1951, US media magnate); F.L.W. (1867–1959, US architect); J.S. (1878–1953, Russian political leader); D.R. (1886–1957, Mexican muralist); I.N. (1896–1958, Hungarian leader executed following 1956 revolution); G.O. (1903–50, UK author); A.T. (1912–54, UK computing pioneer); E.P. (1919–52, Argentine political figure).

9

Here are nine literary classics from the decade, but can you identify the author of each? *Ideas and Opinions*, *Tristes Tropiques*, *Doctor Zhivago*, *Fahrenheit 451*, *I, Robot*, *Kon-Tiki*, *Lolita*, *The Captive Mind* and *On the Road*.

10

Which ten films won the Best Picture Oscar between 1950 and 1959?

11

Which countries did the following figures lead during the 1950s? Adolfo Ruiz, Alcide De Gasperi, Éamon de Valera, Faisal II, Josip Broz Tito, King Idris, Konrad Adenauer, John Diefenbaker, Nikita Khrushchev, Robert Menzies, Tage Erlander and Urho Kekkonen.

Answers on page 160

Famous People I

1

Which ancient Egyptian's tomb was famously discovered by Howard Carter in 1922?

2

What were the names of the victims in the notorious O. J. Simpson murder trial?

3

Who were the three members of Rome's First Triumvirate?

4

Who wrote the four New Testament gospels?

5

Who was in the original Jackson 5 line-up?

6

Who were the first six women to go into space?

7

To which famous figures were the following married? Amenhotep IV (Akhenaten), Marie Antoinette, Mary Shelley, Pocahontas, Queen Mumtaz Mahal, Robert Browning and Wallis Simpson.

8

Can you identify the eight companies from their founders and year of foundation? J. C. Jacobsen (1847); Sir Thomas Sutherland (1865); Yataro Iwasaki (1870); David H. McConnell (1886); John Pemberton and Asa Candler (1892); Charles Coffin, Edwin Houston, Elihu Thomson and Thomas Edison (1892); Adolf Dassler (1924); Richard Branson (1972).

9

Nine US vice presidents have assumed the presidency on the death or resignation of the president. Can you name them all?

10

Identify the explorers from the clues. Captain who claimed east coast of Australia for Britain; Spanish explorer known for claiming the Aztec Empire in the sixteenth century; Chinese explorer who made seven voyages to Indian Ocean between 1405 and 1433; Italian-born explorer after whom 'America' is said to be named; Italian who lived at Kublai Khan's court; Dutch discoverer of New Zealand; man credited with discovering America; favourite of Elizabeth I whose American explorations didn't prevent his execution; first person to circumnavigate the world, despite dying before docking back in Spain; Scottish missionary who became first European to see Victoria Falls.

11

Here are the birthnames of fifteen famous people, but how are they better known? Frederick Austerlitz, Norma Jeane Baker, Frances Gumm, Caryn Johnson, Allen Konigsberg, Ehrich Weiss, Marion Morrison, Edson Arantes do Nascimento, François-Marie Arouet, Julia Wells, Carlos Irwin Estévez, Nicolas Coppola, Audrey Ruston, Sofia Scicolone and Jean-Baptiste Poquelin.

Answers on page 161

The Arts I

1

What did Vincenzo Peruggia notoriously steal in 1911?

2

In Raphael's famous fresco, *The School of Athens*, which two philosophers stand together beneath the archway at its centre?

3

In which centuries were the following artworks created? *The Beheading of Saint John the Baptist* (Caravaggio), *The Starry Night* (Vincent van Gogh), *Venus of Urbino* (Titian).

4

In which operas do these villains appear? Barnaba, the Duke of Mantua, Peter Quint and Scarpia.

5

Who painted the following five great works? *American Gothic*, *The Arnolfini Marriage*, *Dance at Le Moulin de la Galette*, *Guernica* and *The Night Watch*.

6

Who composed each of these ballets? *Swan Lake* (1876), *Giselle* (1841), *Romeo & Juliet* (1938), *The Firebird* (1910), *La Bayadère* (1877) and *A Midsummer Night's Dream* (1962).

7

Where can you find the following great works of art? *Les Demoiselles d'Avignon* (Pablo Picasso), *The Birth of Venus* (Sandro Botticelli), *Book of Kells*, *The Garden of Earthly Delights* (Hieronymus Bosch), *The Last Judgement* (Michelangelo), *The Last Supper* (Leonardo da Vinci) and *Mona Lisa* (Leonardo da Vinci).

8

Which eight artists inspired the following movies? *The Agony and the Ecstasy*, *Big Eyes*, *Frida*, *Girl with a Pearl Earring*, *Lust for Life*, *Mr Turner*, *My Left Foot* and *Séraphine*.

9

According to Hesiod, what were the names of the nine Greek muses?

10

From which countries did or do the following artists come? Ai Weiwei, Edvard Munch, Frida Kahlo, Gustav Klimt, Jackson Pollock, Michelangelo, Rembrandt, René Magritte, Salvador Dalí and Wassily Kandinsky.

11

Can you recall all of Gilbert and Sullivan's fourteen operettas?

Answers on page 162

Up in the Sky

1

Which bird features on the Great Seal of the United States?

2

The supersonic airliner, Concorde, was the result of a joint project between which two nations?

3

Which are the three largest birds by wingspan?

4

What are the four major types of cloud?

5

Earth's atmosphere is divided into five basic categories on the basis of height above the planet's surface. What are they?

6

Ratites are a genus of large, flightless birds, including ostriches. Can you name the other six major breeds included in the group?

7

A rainbow is made up of which seven colours?

8

Can you identify these eight famous aviators from the descriptions? Known as Red Baron; first American to orbit the Earth; first woman to fly solo across the Atlantic Ocean; wealthy aviation pioneer and builder of the 'Spruce Goose'; first person to fly solo non-stop around the world in a hot air balloon; brothers who invented the first practical hot air balloon; travelled from New York to Paris in the Spirit of St Louis; captain of the Enola Gay.

9

Which are the moon's largest seas (each with a diameter in excess of 500 km)?

10

What are the ten brightest stars as seen from Earth?

11

Can you identify the celebrities who lost their lives in air crashes from the clues below (initials, lifespan and description)? R.A., 1872–1928, Norwegian explorer; S.C.B., 1897–1945, Indian nationalist leader; A.J., 1903–41, aviation pioneer; D.G., 1905–61, Swedish Secretary-General of the United Nations; R.M., 1923–69, American boxer; B.H., 1936–59, American singer; O.R., 1941–67, American singer; S.F., 1944–2007, American adventurer; L.K., 1949–2010, President of Poland; S.R.V., 1954–90, American blues guitarist; H.C., 1969–2002, South African cricket captain; A., 1979–2001, American entertainer.

Answers on page 164

Food and Drink I

1

Which popular Portuguese delicacy was invented by Catholic monks at the Jerónimos Monastery?

2

A turducken consists of meat from a duck and which two other birds?

3

What are Australia's three major wine regions by volume?

4

In which countries did these cakes originate? Baumkuchen, croquembouche, Dobos torte and genoise.

5

In a classic Margherita pizza, what are the five ingredients used in the topping?

6

Can you identify the foods from these six Indian terms? Aloo, dhal, gobi, murgh, paneer and sag.

7

From which countries do the following spice mixes come? Bumbu, Cajun, five-spice powder, jerk spice, mixed spice, quatre épices and shichimi togarashi.

8

Which nations produce the most of the following foodstuffs? Casava, cocoa, coffee, figs, olives, saffron, turkey and wheat.

9

With which food or drink are the following fictional characters particularly associated? Garfield, Homer Simpson, James Bond, Jean-Luc Picard, Kojak, Paddington Bear, Popeye, the Teenage Mutant Ninja Turtles and Winnie the Pooh.

10

Identify the cocktails from their ingredients (according to International Bartenders' Association). Vodka, tomato juice, lemon juice; gin, Heering cherry liqueur, Cointreau, DOM Bénédictine, grenadine, pineapple juice, lemon juice, angostura bitters; vodka, tequila, white rum, triple sec, gin, lemon juice, Gomme syrup, cola; white rum, lime juice, mint, sugar, soda water; tequila, Cointreau, lemon juice; vodka citron, Cointreau, lime juice, cranberry juice; vodka, Galliano, orange juice; vodka, orange juice; vodka, coffee liqueur, cream; rye, sweet red vermouth, angostura bitters, maraschino cherry.

11

From which countries do these seventeen beer brands hail? Asahi, Brahma, Carlsberg, Castle Lager, Cerveza Quilmes, Chang, Chimay, Coors Light, Harbin, Heineken, Kingfisher, Modelo, Molson, Peroni, Pilsner Urquell Czech Republic, Victoria Beer and Żywiec.

Answers on page 165

Politics

1

What was the name of the White House intern with whom Bill Clinton was accused in 1998 of having an affair?

2

Following independence in 1947, who was Pakistan's first governor-general and India's first prime minister?

3

In many nations, such as the USA, governmental authority is divided into which three branches?

4

Which international organizations are known by the following acronyms: ICC, IMF, NATO and OECD?

5

Which five nations have permanent seats on the United Nations Security Council?

6

The United Nations also operates six official languages. What are they?

7

The G7 group of advanced economies comprises which nations?

8

Which eight countries signed up to the Warsaw Pact?

9

In which cities would you find the following royal or imperial palaces? Versailles, Palazzo Pitti, the Alhambra, Schönbrunn Palace, Winter Palace, the Forbidden City, Topkapi Palace, the Amber Fort and Holyrood Palace.

10

In which countries would you find the following legislative bodies: Althingi, Bundestag, Dáil, House of Lords, Knesset, Lok Sabha, Pontifical Commission, Riksdag, Sejm and State Duma.

11

Prior to the UK's exit, which 27 other countries were members of the European Union?

Answers on page 166

Asia

1

Which Indian cricketing legend holds the record for most Test runs?

2

What are the names of the two longest rivers in Asia?

3

Which three cities make up the corners of India's 'golden triangle'?

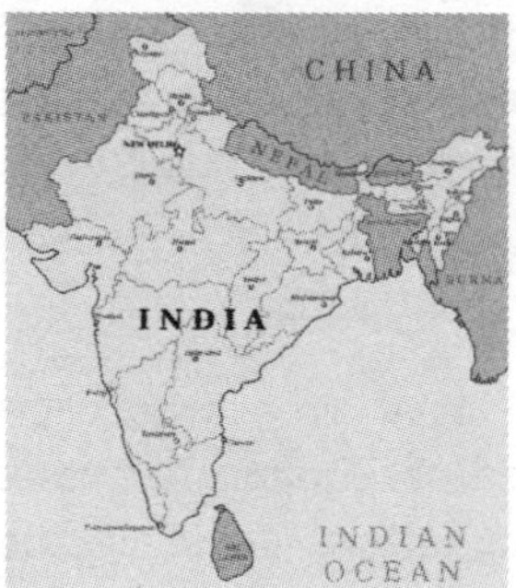

4

Which are the four main islands of Japan?

5

Who wrote these regional literary classics? *Diary of a Madman* (1918), *Wild Swans: Three Daughters of China* (1991), *The Wind-Up Bird Chronicle* (1994), *A Fine Balance* (1995) and *The God of Small Things* (1997).

6

Using the International Organization for Standardization's two-letter coding system, which countries are represented by the codes BT, IQ, KG, KP, SG and YE?

7

What are India's seven largest states by area?

8

In which countries would you find the eight following attractions? Angkor Wat, Borobudur, Heian Shrine, Intramuros, Raffles Hotel, the Red Fort, Ulleungdo Island and Victoria Peak.

9

Which countries did the following nine individuals lead? Deng Xiaoping, Hirohito, Hussein bin Talal, Indira Gandhi, Nursultan Nazarbayev, Pol Pot, Saparmurat Niyazov, Suharto and Than Shwe.

10

Can you name the capital cities of the following ten countries? Azerbaijan, Bangladesh, Bhutan, Cambodia, Laos, Mongolia, Myanmar (Burma), Nepal, the Philippines and Vietnam.

11

China is divided into provinces, municipalities, autonomous regions and special administrative regions. Can you name the four municipalities, five autonomous regions and two special administrative regions?

Answers on page 167

Language

1

What is the traditional sacred language of Hinduism?

2

In a quote widely attributed to George Bernard Shaw, what are said to be 'divided by a common language'?

3

What are Belgium's three official languages?

4

The Greek alphabet begins with alpha and beta, but what are the next four letters?

α β

5

What are the traditional 'five Ws' of journalism?

6

What are the six languages with most native speakers in Asia?

7

What do the following text-speak acronyms stand for? AAMOF, IKR, ILY, IMO, LOL, ROFL, SMH.

8

A demonym is the name given to the resident of any given locality. Can you provide the demonyms for the following eight cities? Bologna, Cambridge, Cape Town, Florence, Ho Chi Minh City, Las Vegas, Moscow and Naples.

9

There are nine sovereign nations where Portuguese is an official language. Can you name them?

10

What are the ten letters on the top line of a standard keyboard?

11

The NATO Phonetic Alphabet begins with alpha and bravo, but can you recall the rest?

Answers on page 169

The 1960s

1

By what name was the Berlin Wall's most famous crossing point known in the West?

2

Which artists created the iconic PopArt pieces 'Whaam!' and 'Campbell's Soup Cans'?

3

Which cities hosted the Summer Olympic Games of 1960, 1964 and 1968?

4

Can you identify these *Time* magazine Persons of the Year from the year and initials? 1961 (JFK), 1963 (MLK), 1964 (LBJ) and 1965 (WW).

5

A legendary animated Great Dane made his debut in a Hanna-Barbera production in 1969, but what was his name and who were the other four original members of his gang?

6

Who did the following six people marry (year of wedding in brackets)? Elizabeth Taylor (1964), Mickey Deans (1965), Mia Farrow (1966), Priscilla Beaulieu (1967), Sharon Tate (1968) and Yoko Ono (1969).

7

In which year did the following take place? Bay of Pigs invasion; Neil Armstrong walks on the moon; Martin Luther King makes 'I have a dream' speech; first successful heart transplant; death of Marilyn Monroe; US troops enter Vietnam; the Prague Spring.

8

Can you name the five members of Pink Floyd, along with the original three members of the the Jimi Hendrix Experience?

9

Here are nine literary classics from the decade, but can you identify the author of each? *The Order of Things*, *The French Lieutenant's Woman*, *Herzog*, *One Hundred Years of Solitude*, *The Prime of Miss Jean Brodie*, *The Master and Margarita*, *Slaughterhouse-Five*, *The Tin Drum* and *Wide Sargasso Sea*.

10

Which ten films won the Best Picture Oscar between 1960 and 1969?

11

Which countries did the following figures lead during the 1960s? Aldo Moro, Alexander Dubcek, Eduardo Frei Montalva, Gamal Abdel Nasser, Harold Holt, Jan de Quay, Julius Nyerere, Leonid Brezhnev, Lester Pearson, Patrice Lumumba, Sukarno and Walter Ulbricht.

Answers on page 170

Music II

1

Who composed 'Flight of the Bumblebee'?

2

Which pairing had a hit in 1994 with the song '7 Seconds'?

3

With which instruments were Stéphane Grappelli, Django Reinhardt and Art Blakey associated?

4

Who was in ABBA?

5

Can you name the original five members of One Direction?

6

The Village People comprise six characters in their classic line-up. What are they?

7

With which movies are these hit songs particularly associated: 'My Heart Will Go On', 'Eye of the Tiger', 'Mrs Robinson', 'Raindrops Keep Fallin' on my Head', 'Let It Go', 'Stayin' Alive' and 'Take My Breath Away'?

8

Who wrote the music for the following eight classic standards: 'Fly Me to the Moon', 'Georgia on My Mind', 'It Don't Mean a Thing (If It Ain't Got That Swing)', 'Moon River', 'New York, New York', 'Night and Day', 'Summertime' and 'White Christmas'?

9

Whose national anthems are these? 'Amhrán na bhFiann', 'Jana Gana Mana', 'Kimigayo', 'La Brabançonne', 'La Marseillaise', 'March of the Volunteers', 'The Thunder Dragon Kingdom', 'There is a Lovely Country', and 'Wilhelmus'.

10

Can you identify the composers of these classical compositions: the *Brandenburg Concertos*, *Carmina Burana*, 'Finlandia', *The Four Seasons*, Hungarian Dances, *The Messiah*, 'Moonlight Sonata', *The Planets*, the *Peer Gynt* Suite and *Pomp and Circumstance*?

11

To 2018, Madonna has released thirteen studio albums and three soundtrack albums. Can you name them?

Answers on page 171

General Knowledge III

1

In which year did Britain hand control of Hong Kong back to China?

2

What were the names of the Muppet pair who heckled performances from their balcony seats?

3

What are the names of Donald Duck's nephews?

4

What are the classical 'four temperaments'?

5

The Portuguese flag features which five colours?

6

German is an official language in which six sovereign nations?

7

Can you name the seven Catholic sacraments?

8

What are the eight biggest moons by volume in our Solar System?

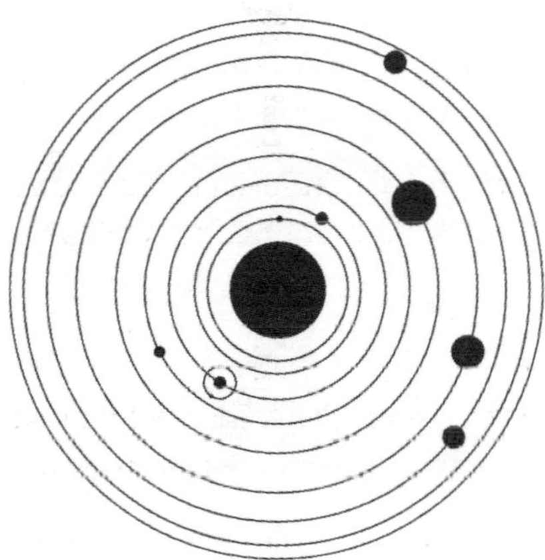

9

Who were the nine members of the classic Addams Family household?

10

At which stadia do the following European football clubs play their home games: Ajax, Barcelona, Bayern Munich, Everton, Glasgow Rangers, Inter Milan, Manchester United, Paris Saint-Germain, Porto and Real Madrid?

11

As of 2018, FIDE, chess's world governing body, has recognized 15 male world champions since 1948. Who?

Answers on page 172

Heroes

1

What is the name of the Korean American artist whose work on the X-Men comic book in 1991 helped it become the bestselling comic book of all time?

2

Can you name the writer and artist duo who created the graphic novel *Watchmen*?

3

Can you name the three Powerpuff Girls?

4

Who are the members of Marvel's Fantastic Four?

5

In Hergé's Tintin stories, what are the names of Tintin's dog, the absent-minded professor, the pipe-smoking sea captain and the two failing detectives?

6

What were the names of the five teenagers chosen to be Mighty Morphin Power Rangers in the show's original series, and what was their mentor called?

7

Who were the seven original members of DC Comics' Justice League?

8

Can you name the four Teenage Mutant Ninja Turtles, their *sensei*, their female human companion, their ice hockey mask-wearing ally and their arch nemesis?

9

Can you name the members of this trio of trios: the Impossibles, the Defenders and the DC Trinity?

10

Which characters have the following actors played in the X-Men movie franchise: Halle Berry, Alan Cumming, Kelsey Grammer, Hugh Jackman, Jennifer Lawrence, James Marsden, Ian McKellen, Anna Paquin, Patrick Stewart and Lucas Till?

11

Can you identify the superheroes from their alterego names: Bruce Wayne, Steve Rogers, Selina Kyle, Bobby Drake, Britt Reid, Bruce Banner, Tony Stark, Max Eisenhardt, Reed Richards, Dick Grayson, Peter Parker, Kara Danvers, Clark Kent, Benjamin Grimm and Diana Prince?

Answers on page 174

Europe

1

Which landlocked nation is bordered by France to the north and Spain to the south?

2

By which two other names was the city of St Petersburg known in the twentieth century?

3

What are the three orders of classical Greek architecture?

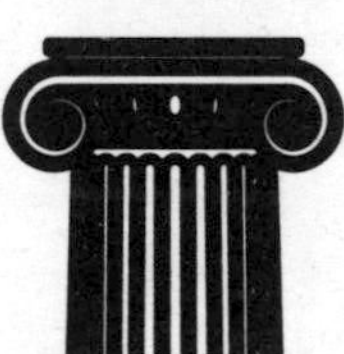

4

Which four national capitals lie on the River Danube?

5

Which five nation states make up the Nordic countries?

6

Which six nations border the Black Sea?

7

Name the European cities in which you'll find these museums and art galleries: Alte Pinakothek, Galleria Borghese, the Musée d'Orsay, the Prado, the Rijksmuseum, the Uffizi Gallery and the Serpentine Galleries.

8

The country of Yugoslavia broke up in the 1990s. This split resulted in seven new nation states, one of whose nations status is disputed, plus an autonomous province. Can you name the new states and the province?

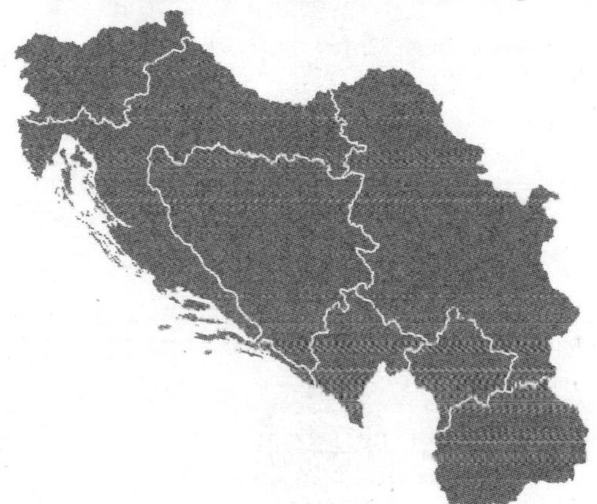

9

Germany is bordered by which nine other countries?

10

Name the capital cities of the following European countries: Albania, Bulgaria, Croatia, Iceland, Latvia, Malta, Norway, Romania, Slovenia and Turkey.

11

Germany is made up of sixteen states (or *Länder*). Can you name them all?

Answers on page 175

Cinema II

1

What was the first feature-length 'talkie' movie, released in 1927?

2

What are the names of the spaceman and the cowboy in the *Toy Story* films?

3

For which three films did Ingmar Bergman win Best Foreign Film Oscars?

4

In the *Godfather* films, who were the four children of Vito Corleone?

5

Which five countries are the world's most prolific film-makers in terms of productions per year?

6

Who directed these classics of French New Wave cinema? *Adieu Philippine*, *Hiroshima Mon Amour*, *Jules et Jim*, *Les Cousins*, *Lola* and *Vivre sa vie*.

7

Who were the seven stars of the 1960 western, *The Magnificent Seven*?

8

Between 1977 and 2017, eight Star Wars movies were released. Can you name them?

9

Can you name the directors of these nine winners of the Palme d'Or award at Cannes? *Amour*, *The Class*, *Dancer in the Dark*, *Farewell My Concubine*, *Paris, Texas*, *The Pianist*, *The Piano*, *The Third Man* and *The Tree of Life*.

10

Can you identify the film from the tagline? A lot can happen in the middle of nowhere; An adventure 65 million years in the making; Check in, relax, take a shower; Don't go in the water; Here's to the fools who dream; His story will touch you, even though he can't; In space no one can hear you scream; The true story of a real fake; What a Glorious Feeling; Who you gonna call?

11

Can you name the 19 films in the first three phases of the Marvel Cinematic Universe (to 2018)?

Answers on page 176

Prizes and Awards

1

Who, in 2014, became the youngest ever recipient of the Nobel Peace Prize?

2

In 1960, which two musicals tied for the Best Musical award at the Tony Awards?

3

Which three films have won the 'big five' Oscars (Best Film, Best Director, Best Actor, Best Actress, Best Screenplay)?

4

Which four individuals have won two Nobel prizes?

5

Beyoncé holds the record for the most MTV Video Music Awards, with twenty-four wins. But who are the next five most successful artists between the awards' inaugural ceremony in 1984 and 2017?

6

What are the six categories of Nobel Prize?

7

Who authored the following Pulitzer Prize for Fiction winners? *The Age of Innocence* (1921), *Gone with the Wind* (1937), *To Kill a Mockingbird* (1961), *Rabbit is Rich* (1982), *Beloved* (1988), *The Shipping News* (1994) and *The Goldfinch* (2014).

8

To 2018, eight men had been awarded the Laureus World Sports Award for Sportsman of the Year. Who are they?

9

Nine men have won two or more Best Actor Academy Awards, but who are they?

10

To 2017, ten people or bands had won twenty-two or more Grammies. Who?

11

With which sports are the following trophies associated? The Ashes, America's Cup, Borg-Warner Trophy, Commissioner's Trophy, Fed Cup, Jules Rimet Trophy, Lance Todd Trophy, Larry O'Brien Trophy, Ryder Cup, Stanley Cup, Thomas Cup, Vince Lombardi Trophy, William Webb Ellis Cup, Woodlawn Vase and the Yellow Jersey.

Answers on page 178

The Olympics

1

In which event did Dick Fosbury develop a revolutionary new technique?

2

Who were the two American athletes sent home from the 1968 Mexico Olympics for giving Black Power salutes during their medal ceremony?

3

In which three years have the Summer Olympics been cancelled?

4

Swimmers compete in which four strokes at the Olympics?

5

What are the colours of the five Olympic rings?

6

Which six events do men compete in during an Olympic gymnastics competition?

7

Including now defunct nations, which seven countries have won the most Winter Olympic medals to 2017?

8

Which eight field events are contested in Olympic athletics?

9

Including now defunct nations, which nine countries have won the most Summer Olympics medals to 2016?

10

Which ten athletic events make up the classic decathlon?

11

What were the host cities for the Summer Olympic Games from the inaugural games in 1896 until those held in 1936?

Answers on page 179

The 1970s

1

What was the popular term given to the thawing of US–Sino relations prompted by the US table tennis team's acceptance of an invitation to visit China?

2

Which cities hosted the Summer Olympic Games of 1972 and 1976?

3

Who were the three members of the band known as ELP?

4

Who were the members of China's so-called 'Gang of Four'?

5

Which women served as head of state or government in the following countries during the decade? Argentina, Central African Republic, India, Israel and the UK.

6

Which countries did the following figures lead during the 1970s? Agostinho Neto, Edward Gierek, Georges Pompidou, José López Portillo, Mengistu Haile Mariam and Zulfikar Ali Bhutto.

7

Can you identify these *Time* magazine Persons of the Year from the year and initials? 1970 (W.B.), 1971 (R.N.), 1972 (H.K.), 1973 (J.S.), 1976 (J.C.), 1977 (A.S.), 1978 (D.X.).

8

Can you identify these eight notable people who died in the decade (initials, dates and professions provided)? P.P. (1881–1973, Spanish artist); C.C. (1883–1971, French fashion designer); E.P. (1885–1972, American poet); C.C. (1889–1977, British star of silent films); A.C. (1890–1976, British crime writer); K.G. (1906–78, Austrian mathematician known for his Incompleteness Theorem); J.H. (1913–75, American union leader); J.J. (1943–70, American singer).

9

Here are nine literary classics from the decade, but can you identify the author of each? *Season of Anomy*, *The Day of the Jackal*, *Gravity's Rainbow*, *If on a Winter's Night a Traveller*, *Orientalism*, *The Periodic Table*, *Roots*, *The Book of Laughter and Forgetting* and *Tinker, Tailor, Soldier, Spy*.

10

Which ten films won the Best Picture Oscar between 1970 and 1979?

11

Who had big hits with these albums of the 1970s? *Arrival*, *Abraxas*, *Bridge Over Troubled Water*, *Exile on Main St*, *Exodus*, *Oxygène*, *Paranoid*, *Un Canto a Galicia*, *Rumours*, *Songs in the Key of Life*, *Trans-Europa Express* and *Wish You Were Here*.

Answers on page 180

Geography II

1

The Horseshoe Falls, American Falls and Bridal Veil Falls together make up which spectacular natural phenomenon?

2

Lake Titicaca is found on the border of which two countries?

3

Ignoring continental landmasses, can you identify the world's three largest islands by area?

4

What are the four national languages used in Switzerland?

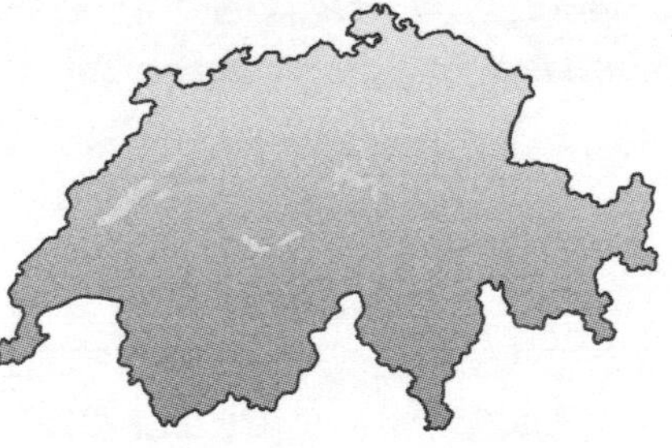

5

Can you name the lines of latitude to be found at: 0°, 66.5° north, 66.5° south, 23.5° north and 23.5° south?

6

Excluding polar deserts, what are the world's six biggest deserts by area?

7

What are the world's seven continents traditionally called?

8

In which countries would you find the following eight natural sites of interest? The Blue Grotto, the Devil's Marbles, the El Tatio geyser field, the Giant's Causeway, the Grand Canyon, Grossglockner, Lake Retba (or Lac Rose) and the Yunnan Stone Forest.

9

In terms of native speakers, which are the nine most widely spoken languages in the world?

10

What are the ten largest countries in the world by area?

11

What are the names of Earth's fifteen primary tectonic plates?

Answers on page 181

The Human Body

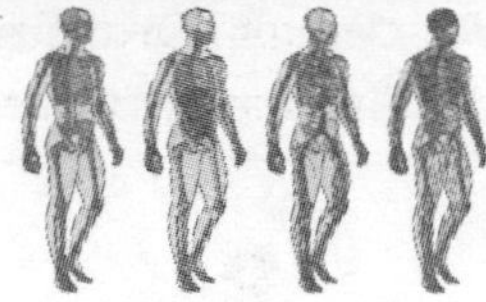

1

Who is considered the first person to completely describe the human circulatory system?

2

By what names are the trachea and larynx commonly referred?

3

What are the three bones in the human ear?

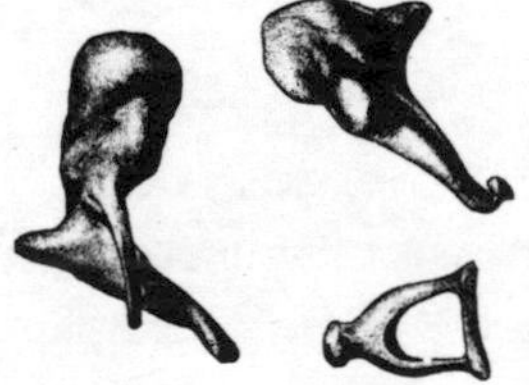

4

Can you name the four different types of teeth in the human mouth?

5

What are the five traditional senses a human possesses?

6

Can you name the six types of freely movable joint in humans?

7

According to the World Health Organization in 2017, what were the seven leading causes of death worldwide?

8

Whereabouts in the human body would you find the following? Cerebellum, gluteal muscles, mandible, metatarsal, quadricep, scaphoid, talus and renal cortex.

9

What are the human body's nine heaviest organs?

10

Which are the ten longest bones in the human body?

11

Can you identify the twelve distinct parts of the eye from the following descriptions? Watery fluid at front of eyeball; the 'middle layer' of the eye between the tough exterior and light-sensitive interior of the eyeball; lining on the inside of eyelid and outside of the front of the eye; the see-through skin that covers the front of the eye; the coloured part of the eye that controls the amount of light entering; the part that focuses light on to the light-sensitive interior of the eye; transfers visual information to the brain; hole that lets light into the eye; light-sensitive layer that lines the interior of the eye; tough skin that covers the outside of the eyeball; ducts that produce moisture to keep the eye clean and hydrated; jelly-like liquid that fills the larger part of the eyeball.

Answers on page 183

Religion

1

Which religion gained official recognition in Haiti in 2003?

2

According to the Book of Genesis, who were the feuding sons of Adam and Eve?

3

By what names are the Jewish festivals of New Year, the Day of Atonement and the Festival of Lights known?

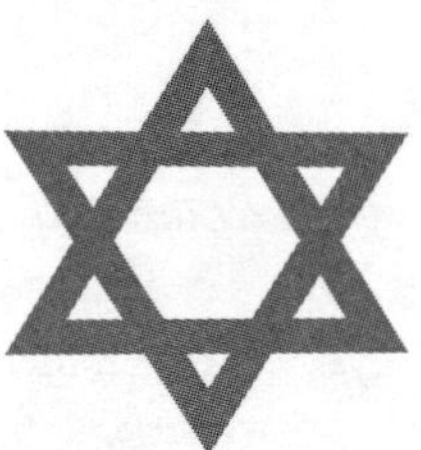

4

What are the Four Noble Truths of Buddhism?

5

What are the Five Pillars of Islam?

6

Can you give the papal names of the last six Popes?

7

What are the seven deadly sins?

8

Can you name the following eight Hindu deities from their descriptions: the Creator, the Preserver, the Destroyer, the god of love and compassion, the goddess of wealth and prosperity, the goddess of war, the elephant god and the monkey king?

9

Can you identify to which religion each of the following sacred texts belong: the Five Classics, the Bhagavad Gita, the Tripitaka, the Tanakh, the Guru Granth Sahib, the Tao Te Ching, the Yasna, the Book of Shadows and the Kojiki?

10

According to the Book of Exodus, what were the ten plagues that befell Egypt?

11

According to Deuteronomy and Judges, what were the original Twelve Tribes of Israel?

Answers on page 184

Musicals I

1

Which musical features the songs 'Food, Glorious Food', 'Oom-Pah-Pah' and 'As Long as He Needs Me'?

2

What are the names of the two lead characters in *Wicked*?

3

In the Oscar-winning film version of *Cabaret*, who played Sally Bowles, her lover Clifford Bradshaw and the Emcee of the Kit Kat Klub?

4

What were the names of the original four 'Pink Ladies' in *Grease*?

5

In the 2002 film version of *Chicago*, what are the names of the characters played by Renée Zellweger, Catherine Zeta-Jones, Richard Gere, Queen Latifah and Christine Baranski?

6

Tim Rice and Andrew Lloyd Webber have worked together on which six musicals?

7

What were the seven von Trapp children called in *The Sound of Music*?

8

Which artists' music inspired these eight musicals: *American Idiot*, *Jersey Boys*, *Mamma Mia!*, *Movin' Out*, *Sunny Afternoon*, *Sunshine on Leith*, *Viva Forever!* and *We Will Rock You*?

9

In which nine musicals do the following songs appear: 'Another Suitcase in Another Hall', 'Defying Gravity', 'Getting To Know You', 'I Could Have Danced All Night', 'It's a Hard Knock Life', 'Luck Be a Lady', 'Oh, What a Beautiful Mornin'', 'Send in the Clowns' and 'You'll Never Walk Alone'?

10

After debuting with *Oklahoma!*, Richard Rodgers and Oscar Hammerstein created ten more musicals together. What were they?

11

Stephen Sondheim has composed eighteen major musicals. Can you name them?

Answers on page 185

Life at Sea

1

Which legendary sea monster, a squid-like creature supposedly living in the waters around Norway, was first described by Erik Pontoppidan in the eighteenth century?

2

When a ship is facing forward, by what terms should you refer to its left and right sides, respectively?

3

In the world of Disney, what was the name of the goldfish in *Pinocchio*, Nemo's father in *Finding Nemo*, and Ariel's best friend in *The Little Mermaid*?

4

Can you identify these famous people who were all lost at sea? You have their initials, nationalities, jobs and dates to help you. B.D., Portuguese explorer, *c.* 1450–1500; H.H., Australian Prime Minister, 1908–67; R.M., Czech-born entrepreneur and media tycoon, 1923–91; N.W., American actress, 1938–81.

5

What are the names of the world's five oceans?

6

Which six fish breeds can hit the highest swim speeds?

7

What are the seven largest shark breeds by length?

8

Which eight countries boast the greatest length of coastline?

9

Can you name the nine deepest ocean trenches?

10

What are the ten largest whale breeds by length?

11

Can you identify these famous vessels from fact and fiction? Captain Ahab's boat in *Moby Dick*; Captain Hook's ship in *Peter Pan*; fabled US ship known as 'Old Ironsides'; Greenpeace research vessel bombed in New Zealand in 1985; Horatio Nelson's flagship at the Battle of Trafalgar; German battleship sunk in May 1941 with the loss of over 1,400 lives; legendary ship captained by Jason; Long John Silver's ship in Robert Louis Stevenson's *Treasure Island*; ocean liner sunk by a German U-boat on 7 May 1915; the name of a ship to feature in the title of one of the Narnia novels; the submarine in Jules Verne's *Twenty Thousand Leagues Under the Sea*; the vessel that transported Dracula to England in Bram Stoker's novel.

Answers on page 186

General Knowledge IV

1

Which enzyme is added to milk in the manufacture of most hard cheeses?

2

In Roman mythology, who were the twin brothers suckled by a she-wolf?

3

What are the three flavours in a Neapolitan ice cream?

4

Teams from the USA and which four other countries have won the Americas Cup in sailing from the first contest in 1851 until 2018?

5

What was the original line-up of Marvel's Avengers?

6

What are the six categories of question in the classic version of Trivial Pursuit?

7

Can you name the highest mountain in each of Africa, Asia, North America, South America, Antarctica, continental Australia and Europe?

8

By what stage names are the following eight rappers better known: Andre Romelle Young, Armando Christian Pérez, Calvin Broadus Jr, Christopher Wallace, Curtis James Jackson III, Marshall Mathers III, Shawn Carter and Tracy Marrow?

9

What are the first nine prime numbers?

10

What do the Ten Commandments say?

11

If you suffered with the following phobias, what would you fear? Acrophobia, aerophobia, agoraphobia, arachnophobia, coulrophobia, gynophobia, musophobia, ophidiophobia, phasmophobia, phobophobia, somniphobia and trypanophobia.

Answers on page 188

The 1980s

1

In Nintendo's legendary arcade game, Mario Bros, what was Mario's brother called?

2

What was the name of the president of the Philippines who fled the country in 1986, along with his shoe-loving wife?

3

Which cities hosted the Summer Olympic Games in 1980, 1984 and 1988?

4

Can you identify these *Time* magazine Persons of the Year from the year and initials? 1981 (L.W.), 1983 (Y.A.), 1986 (C.A.), 1989 (M.G.).

5

Which five people were in the Guns N' Roses line-up for the recording of their breakthrough *Appetite for Destruction* album?

6

Which countries did the following figures lead during the 1980s? Ayatollah Ali Khamenei, Helmut Kohl, Hosni Mubarak, P. W. Botha, Yitzhak Shamir and Yuri Andropov.

7

In which years did the following events take place? Pope John Paul II is shot; the Berlin Wall falls; the Challenger space shuttle explodes on take-off; a major gas leak occurs in Bhopal, India; Sally Ride becomes the first American woman in space; video game Pac-Man is introduced; Haiti's Baby Doc is removed from power in a coup.

8

Can you identify these eight notable people who died in the decade (initials, dates and professions provided)? J.M. (1893–1983, Spanish artist); A.H. (1899–1980, British film director); I.B. (1915–82, Swedish actress); T.M. (1917–82, jazz musician); I.G. (1917–84, Indian political leader); A.S. (1918–81, Egyptian political leader); R.F. (1918–88, American theoretical physicist); D.F. (1932–85, American primatologist).

9

Here are nine literary classics from the decade, but can you identify the author of each? *Norwegian Wood*, *The Lover*, *The Handmaid's Tale*, *Midnight's Children*, *The Name of the Rose*, *Perfume: The Story of a Murderer*, *The Remains of the Day*, *The Unbearable Lightness of Being*, *The House of the Spirits*.

10

Which ten films won the Best Picture Oscar between 1980 and 1989?

11

Who had big hits with these albums of the 1980s? *Born in the USA*, *Brothers in Arms*, *Doolittle*, *Graceland*, *Look Sharp!*, *Hunting High and Low*, *Hysteria*, *Immigrés*, *No Jacket Required*, *Purple Rain*, *Raw Like Sushi*, *True Blue*.

Answers on page 189

Literature II

1

What was Vikram Seth's 1993 epic novel set in post-partition India called?

2

Margaret Mitchell's *Gone with the Wind* tells the story of which plantation owner's daughter, and to whom is she married at the end of the book?

3

What were the names of the *Three Musketeers* in the novel by Robert Dumas?

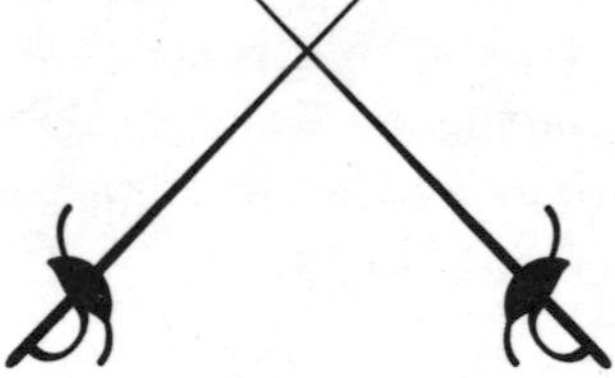

4

What were the four March sisters called in Louisa May Alcott's *Little Women*?

5

What are the names of the eponymous Famous Five in Enid Blyton's stories?

6

Who were the crime-fighting stars of the following novels: *The Maltese Falcon*, *Last Bus to Woodstock*, *The Name of the Rose*, *The Big Sleep*, *Faceless Killers* and *The Murders in the Rue Morgue*.

7

As of 2018, George R. R. Martin's *A Song of Ice and Fire* series was expected to finish with publication of the seventh novel in the cycle. What are the titles of all seven novels?

8

By which pen names are the following authors better known? Charles Lutwidge Dodgson, Georges Remi, Józef Teodor, Konrad Korzeniowski, Howard Allen Frances O'Brien, Erika Mitchell, Eric Blair, Mary Anne Evans and Theodor Seuss Geisel.

9

Can you name the world's nine biggest libraries, in terms of volumes held?

10

Who wrote the books on which these films were based: *A Clockwork Orange*, *Atonement*, *Breakfast at Tiffany's*, *The Color Purple*, *Doctor Zhivago*, *The English Patient*, *The Godfather*, *One Flew Over the Cuckoo's Nest* and *The Silence of the Lambs*?

11

Can you name the thirteen novels and novellas of Leo Tolstoy?

Answers on page 190

North America

1

Where would you find the city of Tegucigalpa?

2

Which Canadian sprinter was disqualified from the 1988 Olympic Games, having crossed the line first in the men's 100 metres? And who consequently gained the gold?

3

What are the three 'unalienable rights' cited in the US Declaration of Independence?

4

What are the names of Mexico's four most populous cities?

5

Can you name the five Great Lakes of North America?

6

Can you name the six Caribbean nations of which these cities are the capital? Bridgetown, Nassau, Port of Spain, Roseau, Santo Domingo and St. John's.

7

As of 2018, which seven Canadian teams play in the National Hockey League?

8

What are the names of the eight Ivy League universities?

9

What are the nine largest cities in the USA by population?

10

Can you name Canada's ten provinces?

11

What were the original thirteen British colonies in North America that declared their independence in 1776 and formed the United States?

Answers on page 192

Mythology

1

Which ancient belief system, according to some interpretations, predicted the end of the world for 21 December 2012.

2

What are the titles of Homer's two great epics of Greek mythology?

3

Who, respectively, were the Egyptian sun god, the goddess of fertility and magic, and the god of the dead?

4

In Roman mythology, who, respectively, were the king of the gods, the goddess of the hearth and home, the goddess of love and the messenger of the gods?

5

What are the titles of the five books in Rick Riordan's Percy Jackson & the Olympians series?

6

Can you finish off the titles of these fables by Aesop?
The Bear and the ________; The Hare and the ________;
The Kite and the ________; The Monkey and the ________;
The Thief and the ________; The Wolf in ________.

7

Can you identify the mythical creatures from these clues? Body of a bird and head of a woman; body of a lion and head and wings of an eagle; half human and half horse; half man and half goat; head of a woman and torso and tail of a fish; single-horned horse; winged horse.

8

Who are the eight Immortals of Chinese mythology?

9

Can you name the nine realms of Norse mythology?

10

Can you name the Greek gods of the sea, the Underworld, war, music and archery, fire, wine, and sleep, as well as the goddesses of war and wisdom, childbirth, and hunting.

11

Can you name the twelve signs of the Chinese zodiac?

Answers on page 193

Plants and Trees

1

Which flower prompted a notorious speculation bubble in the seventeenth century?

2

What are the terms for plants that go through their complete life cycle in a single growing season, and those that persist for many seasons?

3

Which woods and forests featured in the following literary works: *Winnie-the-Pooh*, *The Adventures of Robin Hood* and *Star Wars*.

4

What are the names for the following parts of a flower. The pollen-producing part; the 'female' part; the part that attracts insects; the part that supplies nutrients from the soil.

5

Complete the book titles, each missing a flower. The Black ________ (James Ellroy); ________ Miller (Henry James); The ________ Eaters (Tatjana Soli); The Name of the ________ (Umberto Eco); Under the ________ (Louisa M. Alcott).

6

With which sorts of tree are the following people particularly associated? Buddha, Anne Frank, General Sherman, George Washington, Isaac Newton and Joseph of Arimathea.

7

Can you identify the common names of these seven trees from their Latin names? *Acer*, *betula*, *castanea*, *fraxinus*, *populus*, *pinus* and *quercus*.

8

Which eight countries contain the most forest by area?

9

Which fruits or nuts flavour these liquors? Chambord, crème de cassis, Cointreau, perry, amaretto, limoncello, Frangelico, maraschino and Midori.

10

Identify these flowers from their Latin names. *Antirrhinum*, *centaurea*, *dianthus*, *digitalis*, *helianthus*, *impatiens*, *lathyrus*, *syringa*, *galanthus* and *gypsophila*.

11

In which cities would you find the following famous gardens? Beihai Park, Boboli Gardens, Central Park, Chapultepec, Djugarden, Englischer Garten, Hyde Park, Jardin du Luxembourg, Kings Park and Botanical Garden, Lumpini Park, Namba Parks, Park Güell, Parque Ibirapuera, Phoenix Park, Stanley Park and Ueno Park.

Answers on page 194

Space

1

Of what celestial phenomenon are Halley's, Hale–Bopp and Hyakutake famous examples?

2

What are Mars's two moons called?

3

Who were the three members of the legendary Apollo 11 crew?

4

What are the four component parts of a comet?

5

Which five major space agencies participate in the International Space Station?

6

What were the six NASA space shuttles called?

7

Which seven gases are the major constituents of dry air on Earth?

8

What, in order of distance from the Sun, are the names of the eight known planets in the solar system?

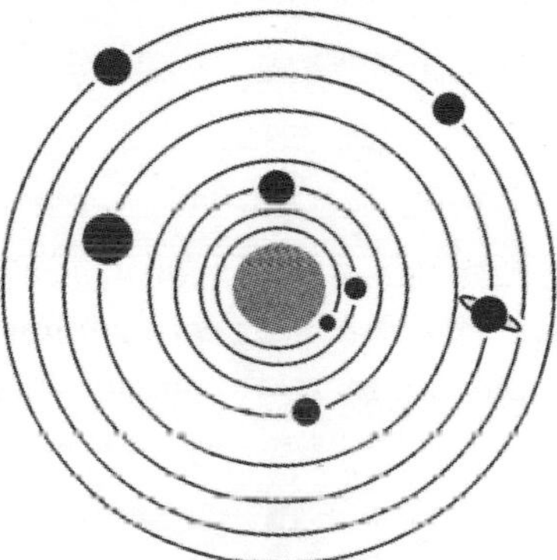

9

Who were the nine main characters in the first series of *Star Trek: The Next Generation*?

10

Aside from the two Apollo 11 members who walked on the moon, which ten other individuals have done so?

11

What are the twelve zodiac constellations?

Answers on page 196

Cities

1

In which country is the city of Timbuktu situated?

2

What are the northernmost and southernmost capital cities on the globe?

3

Can you name the three cities that served as their respective national capitals immediately before Moscow, Belmopan and Abuja?

4

What are the four capitals of the constituent countries of Great Britain and Northern Ireland?

5

Can you name the five boroughs that make up New York City?

6

Which six nations have capital cities that begin with the letter 'R'?

7

Can you identify these American cities from their nicknames: Beantown, the Big Apple, the City of Angels, the Magic City, Motor City, Sin City and the Windy City?

8

In which cities would you find the following attractions: statue of Christ the Redeemer, Hagia Sophia, Sagrada Familia, St Basil's Cathedral, St Peter's Basilica, Table Mountain, the Taj Mahal and the Terracotta Army?

9

Can you identify the nine modern cities from their previous names: Bombay, Edo, Constantinople, Kristania, Madras, Peking, Rangoon, Saigon and Salisbury?

10

On which rivers do the following cities lie: Canberra, Buenos Aires, Prague, Cairo, Paris, Baghdad, Rome, Amsterdam, Dublin and Washington, DC?

11

Can you name the countries of which the following cities are the capital: Abuja, Addis Ababa, Beirut, Dakar, Gabarone, Harare, Jakarta, Kingston, Lima, Minsk, Nicosia, Port-au-Prince, Quito, Seoul, Tallinn and Windhoek?

Answers on page 197

Science II

1

Who reputedly died after contracting pneumonia as a result of carrying out research into the effects of freezing on a dead chicken?

2

In the seventeenth century, which two esteemed mathematicians battled for the title of creator of modern calculus?

3

What are the three fundamental components of an atom?

4

What are the four nucleobases of DNA?

5

Four married couples and a father and son have been jointly awarded Nobel prizes from the science categories. Can you name them?

6

What are the six noble gases?

7

Can you identify the constellations from the descriptions? The chained woman, the dragon, the eagle, the great bear, the peacock, the shield and the unicorn.

8

If water boils at 100°C, normal body temperature is 37°C, room temperature is 21°C and the freezing point of water is 0°C, what are the equivalents in Fahrenheit and Kelvins?

9

Who are the authors of these nine landmark scientific works? *A Brief History of Time*, *De Humani Corporis Fabrica (On the Fabric of the Human Body)*, *De Revolutionibus Orbium Coelestium (On the Revolutions of Heavenly Spheres)*, *Dialogue Concerning the Two Chief World Systems*, *Philosophiae Naturalis Principia Mathematica (Mathematical Principles of Natural Philosophy)*, *Silent Spring*, *The Cosmic Connection*, *The Man Who Mistook His Wife for a Hat and Other Clinical Tales* and *The Origin of Species*.

10

Several elements have been named in honour of people. From their abbreviations, can you say whom these elements are named for? Bh, Cm, Es, Fm, Lr, Md, Mt, No, Rf and Rg.

11

What are these 'ologies' the study of? Apiology, cytology, entomology, gynaecology, haematology, lepidopterology, neurology, oncology, osteology, pathology, somnology and toxicology.

Answers on page 198

The 1990s

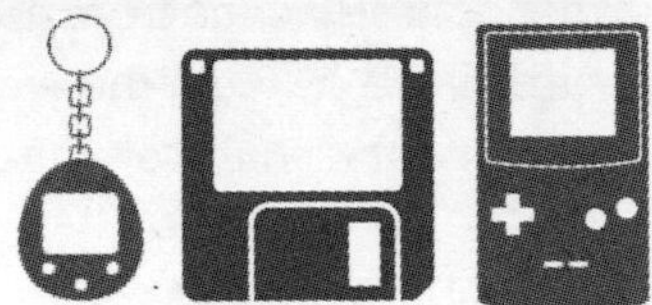

1

Who was the Israeli prime minister assassinated in 1995?

2

Which cities hosted the 1992 and 1996 Summer Olympic Games?

3

Who were the three members of Nirvana?

4

In which years in the 1990s did the following events take place? Princess Diana died in a car crash; Nelson Mandela became president of South Africa; Lance Armstrong won his first Tour de France; the video game Sonic the Hedgehog was released.

5

Who were the five supermodels who appeared in George Michael's iconic 'Freedom! '90' video?

6

Who were the six lead characters in *Friends* called?

7

Seven different men were crowned Formula One world champion during the 1990s. Who were they?

8

In the 1992 film *Reservoir Dogs*, who played the eight characters that carry out a diamond heist?

9

John Grisham published his first novel, *A Time to Kill*, in 1989. Nine more followed in the 1990s. Can you name them?

10

Which ten films won the Best Picture Oscar between 1990 and 1999?

11

Can you name the artists that produced the following albums of the 1990s? *Achtung Baby*, *All Eyez on Me*, *Romanza*, *The Bends*, *Blood Sugar Sex Magik*, *Dangerous*, *Grace*, *Jagged Little Pill*, *Mellow Gold*, *Out of the Time*, *Happy Nation*, *Step by Step*, *Ten*, *Tuesday Night Music Club* and *Aquarium*.

Answers on page 199

Musicals II

1

In which musical did Topol famously play the lead role?

2

What are the names of the two producers in the Mel Brooks' musical, *The Producers*.

3

Which three characters does Dorothy meet on the Yellow Brick Road who accompany her to see the Wizard of Oz?

4

In the 1955 movie version of *Guys and Dolls*, which roles were played by Marlon Brando, Jean Simmons, Frank Sinatra and Vivian Blaine?

5

From the musical *Les Misérables*, name the former prisoner at the centre of the story, the policeman who pursues him, the factory worker who entrusts her daughter to the care of a couple called Thénardier, the Thénardiers' daughter, plus the streetwise urchin who ultimately dies on the revolutionaries' barricade?

6

In his song 'Let's Do It, Let's Fall in Love' (from the musical *Paris*), Cole Porter cited eight bugs and insects that fall in love. Along with ladybugs and fleas, what were the six other types?

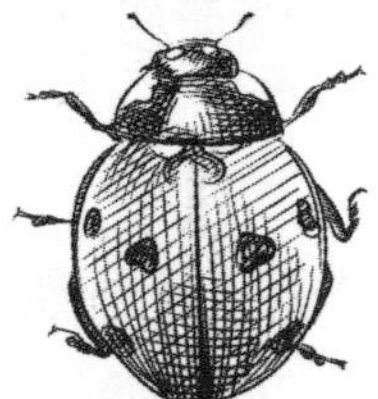

7

In *Seven Brides for Seven Brothers*, what were the names of the seven brothers?

8

In the musical *Cats*, what were the names of: the Theatre Cat, the Mystery Cat, the Railway Cat, the Old Gumbie Cat, the Glamour Cat, the St James's Street Cat, the Bravo Cat and the Conjuring Cat?

9

As of 2017, what were the nine longest-running musicals ever on Broadway?

10

Which ten musicals have won the Best Picture Oscar?

11

In 'My Favourite Things' from *The Sound of Music*, what are the fourteen favourite things described?

Answers on page 200

Food and Drink II

1

What is generally considered the most expensive of all spices?

2

About which green-tinged dish did Dr Seuss famously write?

3

Which three elements constitute the filling of a BLT sandwich?

4

What are the names of the famous Roux brother chefs and their respective chef sons?

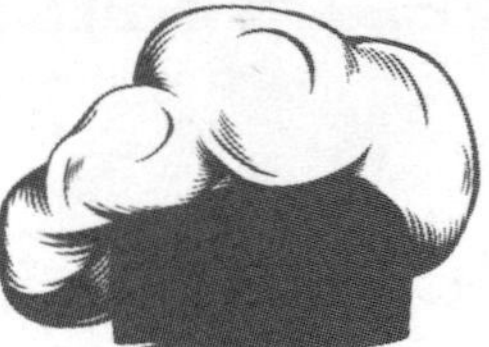

5

What are the five basic flavours that humans can sense?

6

Who wrote the following works of literature with food in the titles? *The Cherry Orchard*, *Chocolat*, *James and the Giant Peach*, *A Clockwork Orange*, *The Grapes of Wrath* and *Fried Green Tomatoes at the Whistle Stop Café*.

7

A regular bottle of champagne holds 75 cl. But by what names are the bottles known that are equivalent to two, four, six, eight, twelve, sixteen and twenty bottles?

8

From which countries do the following cheeses originate? Cotija, Feta, Gouda, Gruyere, Manchego, Monterey Jack, Provolone and Stinking Bishop.

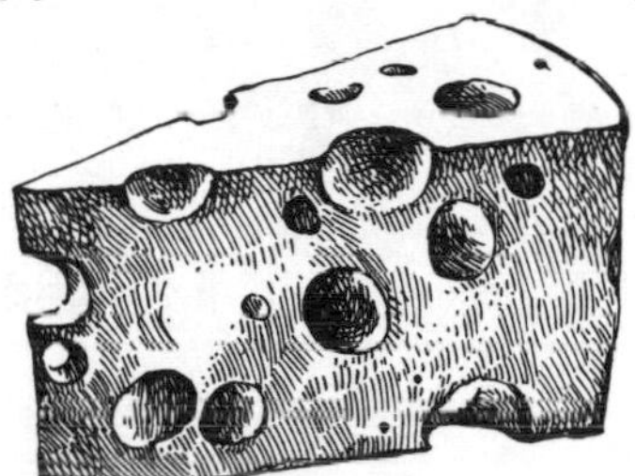

9

Identify the pasta from the rough translation of its name? 'To cut', 'to gobble up', 'grooved', 'little strings', 'little tongues', 'shoestrings', 'small slices', 'spindles' and 'worms'.

10

From which countries do the following breads come? Anpan, bagel, brioche, damper, *Dampfnudel*, dosa, focaccia, mantou, qistibi and tortilla.

11

In which countries did these drinks originate? Absinthe, Amarula, Becherovka, bourbon, Brennivin, calvados, chacha, feni, grappa, Moutai, ouzo, port, sake, sherry, unicum and tequila.

Answers on page 202

Cinema III

1

What is the name of the Mexican film director whose titles include *Cronos* and *Pan's Labyrinth*?

2

In *Casablanca*, what were the first names of the characters played by Humphrey Bogart and Ingrid Bergman?

3

What are the three films that make up Satyajit Ray's landmark of Bengali cinema, *The Apu Trilogy*?

4

To 2018, Meg Ryan and Tom Hanks had starred in which four films together?

5

What are the first five instalments in the *Pirates of the Caribbean* series?

6

What are the six films in the *Alien* franchise released between 1979 and 2017 (and excluding those combining with the *Predator* franchise)?

7

As of 2018, what were the seven highest grossing films from the Japanese Studio Ghibli?

8

Who directed these classics of cinema? *2001: A Space Odyssey*, *Goodfellas*, *La Dolce Vita*, *Mulholland Drive*, *Once Upon a Time in America*, *The Treasure of the Sierra Madre*, *Unforgiven*, *The Wild Bunch*.

9

Can you identify the film from the tagline? To enter the mind of a killer she must challenge the mind of a madman; Does for rock and roll what *The Sound of Music* did for hills; Escape or die frying; He's the only kid ever to get into trouble before he was born; One dream. Four Jamaicans. Twenty below zero; One man's struggle to take it easy; Protecting the Earth from the scum of the universe!; Reality is a thing of the past; The strangest story ever conceived by man.

10

As of 2018, Steven Spielberg has directed ten films that have been nominated for the Best Picture Oscar. Can you name them all?

11

Between 1979 and 2016, there were 13 *Star Trek* movies. Can you name them all?

Answers on page 203

General Knowledge V

1

Which game is often ended by a phrase that derives from the Persian for 'the Shah is helpless'?

2

Which double-act's films included *A Chump at Oxford*, *Block-Heads*, *County Hospital*, *Helpmates* and *Way Out West*?

3

Who are the three members of the animated singing Chipmunks?

4

Which four basic colours are used in the CMYK colour model?

5

Who leant their names to the following dishes? A meringue dessert named after a Russian ballerina; a pizza named after the wife of Umberto I of Italy; a mix of fruit and ice cream named after an Australian operatic soprano; a bread-based snack named for an eighteenth-century English aristocrat; a biscuit named after a nineteenth-century Italian patriot.

6

Since the 1960s, six actors have portrayed Batman on the big screen. Who?

7

Which historical figures feature on US one, two, five, ten, twenty, fifty and 100 dollar bills?

8

Can you name the eight novels produced by Anne, Charlotte and Emily Brontë?

9

Which nine countries are known to have nuclear weapons capabilities?

10

Which ten drivers have, as of 2018, won three or more Formula One world championships?

11

What are the twelve zodiacal birthstones, each associated with a different month of the year?

Answers on page 205

The Arts II

1

Which artist has American crime writer Patricia Cornwell controversially accused of having been Jack the Ripper?

2

Which two sculptors were responsible for the equestrian statue of Gattamelata at Padua and *The Burghers of Calais*?

3

By what names are the artists Michelangelo Merisi, Doménikos Theotokópoulos and Jacopo Comin better known?

4

Which four fashion designers or clothing manufacturers are credited with the creation, respectively, of the bikini, denim jeans, the 'little black dress' and the mini skirt?

5

For which artists did these muses provide inspiration? Camille Claudel, Dora Maar, Edie Sedgwick, Emilie Louise Flöge and Ilona Staller (Cicciolina).

6

With which art movements are the following six artists most closely associated? Claude Monet, Gian Lorenzo Bernini, John Everett Millais, René Magritte, Roy Lichtenstein and Walter Gropius.

7

Can you spot the seven dance styles from the clues? Inextricably linked with the Brazilian carnival; associated with the music of the two Johann Strausses; immortalized in *Saturday Night Fever*; particularly associated with the music of Enrique Jorrín; named after a South Carolina city in the 1920s; features steps such as caminata, baldosa and resolución; street style popularized by the likes of the Rock Steady Crew.

8

In which cities are these theatres and opera houses? The Balboa Theatre, La Scala, Lincoln Center, Margravial Opera House, Palais Garnier, Teatro Colon, the Bolshoi and the Globe Theatre.

9

Can you identify the meanings of the following ballet terms? Plié, grand jeté, arabesque, tour en l'air, assemblé, turn-out, pirouette, croisé and attitude.

10

From which operas do these arias come? 'Casta Diva', 'Che gelida manina', 'Habanera', 'La Donna e Mobile', 'Largo al Factotum', 'Nessun dorma', 'O Fortuna', 'O Mio Babbino Caro', 'Tatiana's Letter' and 'The Queen of the Night'.

11

Who painted these masterpieces? *Landscape with the Fall of Icarus*; *Las Meninas*; *Luncheon of the Boating Party*; *Massacre of the Innocents*; *The Stonemason's Yard*; *The Card Players*; *The Dance Class*; *The Flower Carrier*; *The Persistence of Memory*; *The Scream*; *Water Lilies*; *Yellow–Red–Blue*.

Answers on page 206

Oceania

1

By what alternative name is Uluru known?

2

What are the largest cities on New Zealand's North and South Islands, respectively?

3

What are the emblems of the Australian, Fijian and New Zealand rugby union teams?

4

What are the four biggest of the Hawaiian islands?

5

What are Australia's five longest rivers?

6

Which celebrated Australasian bands produced the albums *Back in Black*, *Fever*, *Kick*, *Murder Ballads*, *Physical* and *Woodface*.

7

In which cities will you find the following stadia: Eden Park, Forsyth Barr Stadium, the Gabba, the MCG, Stadium Australia, the WACA and Westpac Stadium

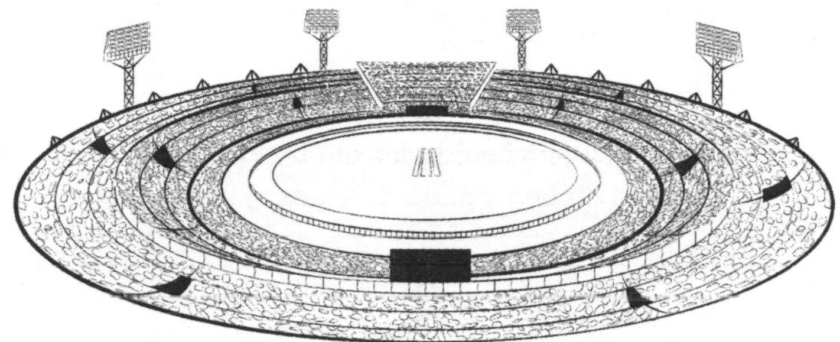

8

Can you name the capitals of each of Australia's eight states and territories?

9

Who wrote these classics of Australasian literature? *Cloudstreet*, *For the Term of His Natural Life*, *The Harp in the South*, *My Brilliant Career*, *Oscar and Lucinda*, *Picnic at Hanging Rock*, *The Power of One*, *The Slap* and *We of the Never Never*.

10

Of which ten Pacific island nations are these cities the capital? Suva, Tarawa, Palikir, Ngerulmud, Port Moresby, Apia, Honiara, Nuku alofa, Funafuti and Port Vila.

11

Can you name all of Australia's fourteen prime ministers from December 1949 up to December 2017?

Answers on page 208

History II

1

Who was the King of the Franks and Lombards who was also crowned Emperor of the Romans in the year 800?

2

Which two nations offered military support to Israel's invasion of Egypt during the 1956 Suez Crisis?

3

Who were the three emperors of the German Empire that existed between 1871 and 1918?

4

AD 69 is known as the Year of the Four Emperors, but who were the quartet who ruled over the Roman Empire that year?

5

Can you identify the famous revolutionaries? Leader of the Cuban Revolution (1953–59); first president of the Republic of China; French Revolutionary whose death signalled the end of the Reign of Terror; revolutionary who became the first president of Algeria in 1963; Venzuelan revolutionary known as the Liberator.

6

Of which countries are these the ruling houses? Alaouite, Grimaldi, Orange-Nassau, Saud, Tupou and Wangchuck.

7

Can you recognize these war leaders from the descriptions? Catholic saint who fought the English in the Hundred Years' War; defeated the Romans at the Battle of Cannae; dying at thirty-three, he extended Greek power as far as the Punjab; German field-marshall known as the Desert Fox; king of Sweden from 1611 and combatant during the Thirty Years' War; sultan of the Ottoman Empire (1520–66); founder of the Mongol Empire.

8

Who were the victims of the following eight assassins? Gavrilo Princip, James Earl Ray, John Bellingham, Lee Harvey Oswald, Leon Czolgosz, Mijailo Mijailovic, Nathuram Godse and Thenmozhi Rajaratnam.

9

Can you name all nine chancellors of the Federal Republic of Germany from 1949 to 2018?

10

Can you name the year in which these landmark peace treaties were signed, and what they signified? The Peace of Westphalia, Treaty of Utrecht, Treaty of Nanjing, Treaty of Shimonoseki, Treaty of Paris, Treaty of Portsmouth, Treaty of Brest-Litovsk, Treaty of Versailles, the Camp David Accords and the Good Friday Agreement.

11

In which year did the following historic events occur? Abolition of slavery in the USA; Battle of Waterloo; beginning of the Spanish civil war; birth of Muhammad; Chernobyl nuclear disaster; Constantine converts to Christianity; execution of English king, Charles I; execution of French king, Louis XVI; foundation of Rome; Germany invaded Russia in the Second World War; Julius Caesar crosses the Rubicon; overthrow of Romanovs in Russia.

Answers on page 209

The 2000s

1

What is the name of the detention camp established off the coast of Cuba by the US government in 2002?

2

Who provided the voices of the eponymous hero and Princess Fiona in the 2001 smash-hit movie, *Shrek*?

3

Which cities hosted the Summer Olympic Games in 2000, 2004 and 2008?

4

What were the names of the four novels in Stephenie Meyer's vampire romance series?

5

Can you identify these *Time* magazine Persons of the Year from the year and initials? R.G. (2001), G.W.B. (2004), Y (2006), V.P. (2007), B.B. (2009).

6

Which countries did the following figures lead during the 2000s? Hamid Karzai, Hu Jintao, Luiz Inácio Lula da Silva, Pervez Musharraf, Silvio Berlusconi and Václav Havel.

7

In which years did the following events take place? Barack Obama is elected President; Usain Bolt breaks the world records for the 100 and 200 metres at the Athletics World Championships in Berlin; Madrid train bombings occur; Wikipedia launches; the Iraq War begins; Pope John Paul II dies; Apple releases the iPhone.

8

Can you identify these eight notable people who died in the decade (initials, dates and professions provided)? L.R. (1902–2003, German filmmaker); B.W. (1906–2002, Austrian-American filmmaker); V.B. (1909–2000, Danish-American musician and comedian); A.M. (1915–2005, American playwright); W.C. (1916–2009, American broadcast journalist); E.K. (1938–2007, American stuntman); S.L. (1954–2004, Swedish writer); S.I. (1962–2006, Australian naturalist).

9

Here are nine literary classics from the decade, but can you identify the author of each? *2666*, *Cloud Atlas*, *Life of Pi*, *My Name is Red*, *The Brief Wondrous Life of Oscar Wao*, *The Corrections*, *The Kite Runner*, *The Road* and *Wolf Hall*.

10

Which ten films won the Best Picture Oscar between 2000 and 2009?

11

Who had big hits with these albums of the 2000s? *Aha Shake Heartbreak*, *American Idiot*, *Back to Black*, *The Blueprint*, *Elephant*, *Funeral*, *Graduation*, *Is This It*, *Kala*, *Kid A*, *A Rush of Blood to the Head* and *Whatever People Say I Am, That's What I'm Not*.

Answers on page 211

Sport II

1

In which sport do *rikishi* compete?

2

Since the Women's Tennis Association introduced computerized rankings in 1975, which two German women have held the number-one spot?

3

In which countries would you find the J1 League, Eredivisie and La Liga football divisions?

4

Which four tournaments make up the Grand Slam in tennis?

5

What are the standard five positions in a basketball team?

6

What are the six ways to score points in American football?

7

The modern heptathlon comprises which seven athletic events?

8

What are the eight standard boxing weight divisions in professional boxing (excluding super and light variants)?

9

As of 2017, which nine teams/franchises could claim four or more baseball World Series wins?

10

Since rankings began in 1986, which ten golfers have held the world number one ranking for the longest as of February 2018?

11

Which twelve football clubs have won the European Cup/UEFA Champions League title more than once since the inaugural final in 1956?

Answers on page 212

Monsters in Fact and Fiction

1

Which monster first appeared on the big screen in a 1954 movie by Ishiro Honda?

2

Who were the two American palaeontologists who became embroiled in the so-called 'Bone Wars'?

3

The three heaviest species of reptiles are all crocodiles, but can you name their specific types?

4

What are the world's four heaviest breeds of snake?

5

What are the titles of the first five movies in the *Jurassic* franchise, released between 1993 and 2018?

6

From which countries did the following horror films originate? *Ringu* (1998), *The Blair Witch Project* (1999), *The Descent* (2005), *Let the Right One In* (2008), *We Are What We Are* (2010), *The Babadook* (2014) and *Train to Busan* (2016).

7

In terms of causing human fatalities, what are the world's seven most dangerous animal species?

8

In which movies (or movie franchises) do these monstrous characters appear? Chucky, Freddy Krueger, Ghostface, Hannibal Lecter, Jason Voorhees, Leatherface, Michael Myers and Pinhead.

9

Identify the mythical beasts from the descriptions. Ape-like Himalayan creature; Oedipus solved his riddle; hairy, man-like creature found in North America; firebreather killed by Bellerophon; human figure made of clay in Jewish legend; serpentine giant killed by Zeus; 'fairy woman' who heralds death of a relative; snake-haired monster with a stony gaze; sea serpent killed by Heracles.

10

Which authors created these literary monsters? Count Dracula, Cthulhu, Frankenstein's Monster, the Gruffalo, the Hound of the Baskervilles, the Jabberwocky, Lord Voldemort, Mr Hyde, Pennywise and Scylla.

11

Can you spot the dozen dinosaurs from these literal translations of their names? Double-beamed lizard, egg thief, face with three horns, fish lizard, great beast, knife tooth, roofed lizard, speedy robber, terrible claw, tyrant lizard king, well-armoured head, winged finger.

Answers on page 213

Literature III

1

Which Greek tragedian, according to legend, was killed when an eagle dropped a tortoise on his head?

2

In *To Kill a Mockingbird*, what were the nicknames of Atticus Finch's two children?

3

Can you name the three parts into which Dante's *Divine Comedy* is split?

4

What are the four novels in Elena Ferrante's Naples Quartet?

5

Between 2000 and 2017, Dan Brown published five novels in his Robert Langdon series. Can you name them?

6

What were Jane Austen's six published novels?

7

As of 2018, the Italian author Umberto Eco had published seven novels. What are they?

8

Who were the authors of these eight great works of philosophical thought? *Candide, or Optimism*; *Critique of Pure Reason*; *In Praise of Folly*; *Leviathan*; *Mythologies*; *The New Organum*; *The Prince*; *A Vindication of the Rights of Women*.

9

What are the names of the original nine Great Houses that rule over Westeros in *Game of Thrones* (the television series inspired by the *A Song of Ice and Fire* cycle of novels)?

10

Who are the authors of these classics of literature? *The Heart of the Matter*, *The Temple of the Golden Pavilion*, *On the Road*, *A Passage to India*, *Madame Bovary*, *Shantaram*, *The Trial*, *The Idiot*, *Kiss of the Spider Woman* and *Vile Bodies*.

11

Name the first 13 novels in James Patterson's Alex Cross series.

Answers on page 215

Famous People II

1

To whom was Joséphine de Beauharnais married?

2

Who was the incumbent French president who married in 2008 and what was the name of his singer-songwriter/model wife?

3

Who were the three members of the classic Destiny's Child line-up?

4

Who were the four members of the classic Led Zeppelin line-up?

5

Who were the original five members of New Kids on the Block?

6

Which actors played the six Avengers characters in the 2012 film directed by Joss Whedon?

7

Can you name all seven of the recording Osmond siblings?

8

Which eight celebrated figures said these words?
'Better to remain silent and be thought a fool
than to speak out and remove all doubt.'
'Darkness cannot drive out darkness: only light can do
that. Hate cannot drive out hate: only love can do that.'
'I came, I saw, I conquered.'
'I think; therefore I am.'
'If I have seen further it is by standing on the shoulders of giants.'
'Many of life's failures are people who did not realize
how close they were to success when they gave up.'
'The unexamined life is not worth living.'
'There is not a Black America and a White
America and Latino America and Asian America
– there's the United States of America.'

9

Can you name the first nine presidents of the United States?

10

Who are the authors of these famous autobiographies?
A Long Walk to Freedom, *De Profundis*, *Dreams from My Father*, *I Know Why the Caged Bird Sings*, *Mein Kampf*, *Moonwalk*, *My Experiments with Truth*, *Out of Africa*, *Good-Bye to All That* and *The Road Ahead*.

11

What were the names of Christ's original twelve apostles?

Answers on page 216

Music III

1

Who wrote the lyrics to 'My Way'?

2

With which countries, respectively, do you associate the balalaika and the koto?

3

For making which instruments are the following most famous? Stradivarius, Steinway and Fender?

4

Who were the four members of R.E.M.?

5

With which instruments are the following musicians most closely associated? Yo-yo Ma, Lang Lang, Yehudi Menuhin, Andrés Segovia and Georges Barrère.

6

Which music stars starred in the movies *8 Mile*, *Desperately Seeking Susan*, *Moonstruck*, *Purple Rain*, *The Bodyguard* and *The Wiz*?

7

Who scored the following Eurovision victories? 'Puppet on a String' (United Kingdom, 1967); 'All Kinds of Everything' (Ireland, 1970); 'Waterloo' (Sweden, 1974); 'Ne Partez Pas Sans Moi' (Switzerland, 1988); 'Diva' (Israel, 1998); 'Hard Rock Hallelujah' (Finland, 2006); 'Rise Like a Phoenix' (Austria, 2014).

8

Here are eight artists who have enjoyed great solo success, but with which bands did they rise to fame? Annie Lennox, Belinda Carlisle, Debbie Harry, Diana Ross, Don Henley, George Michael, Peter Gabriel and Sting.

9

Who composed the following famous film scores? *Breakfast at Tiffany's*, *Enter the Dragon*, *A Fistful of Dollars*, *Gone with the Wind*, *The Great Escape*, *The Lion King*, *A Little Romance*, *Star Wars* and *The Umbrellas of Cherbourg*.

10

Can you identify the Italian musical terms from the following definitions? The end of a piece; the words to an opera, musical or ballet; moderately fast; becoming louder; becoming softer; very loud; sung without instrumental accompaniment; with love; subdued; leading female role in a performance.

11

The modern Symphony Orchestra is divided into strings, woodwind, brass and percussion, but which instruments will you normally find in each section?

Answers on page 217

South America

1

What are the vast large, treeless plains that stretches across Uruguay and parts of Argentina and Brazil called?

2

For which two Spanish clubs did Argentine footballing legend Diego Maradona play?

3

The equator passes through which three South American countries?

4

Can you identify the four South American culinary delicacies from the clues? A meaty black bean stew from Brazil; a stuffed bread or pastry, its name means 'to wrap in bread'; a marinade or sauce for meat, which comes in red and green forms and includes parsley, garlic and oregano; Peruvian doughnut made with sweet potato and squash/pumpkin.

5

Using the International Organization for Standardization's two-letter coding system, which countries are represented by the codes BO, GY, PY, SR and UY.

6

These airports serve which cities? Comodoro Arturo Merino Benítez International Airport, El Dorado International Airport, Guarulhos International Airport, Jorge Chávez International Airport, Jorge Newbery Airport and Simón Bolívar International Airport.

7

Which countries did the following lead? Alberto Fujimori, Augusto Pinochet, Daniel Ortega, Hugo Banzer, Hugo Chávez, Juan Perón and Juscelino Kubitschek.

8

In which countries would you find these eight tourist attractions? The Amazon Theatre, Angel Falls, Cotopaxi National Park, Machu Picchu, Mount Roraima, Perito Moreno Glacier, Punta del Este and Salar de Uyuni.

9

Who wrote these classics of South American literature? *Conversation in the Cathedral*, *The Death of Artemio Cruz*, *Labyrinths*, *Love in the Time of Cholera*, *The Alchemist*, *The Savage Detectives*, *The Labyrinth of Solitude*, *The Motorcycle Diaries* and *Twenty Love Poems and a Song of Despair*.

10

As of 2018, who are the ten Brazilian footballers who have scored during normal or extra-time in FIFA World Cup finals?

11

Name the capitals of Argentina, Bolivia, Brazil, Chile, Colombia, Ecuador, Guyana, Paraguay, Peru, Suriname, Uruguay and Venezuela.

Answers on page 219

Technology and Innovation

1

What was the name of the rocket Elon Musk launched in January 2018?

2

Who were the two principal combatants in the so-called 'War of the Currents' in the nineteenth century?

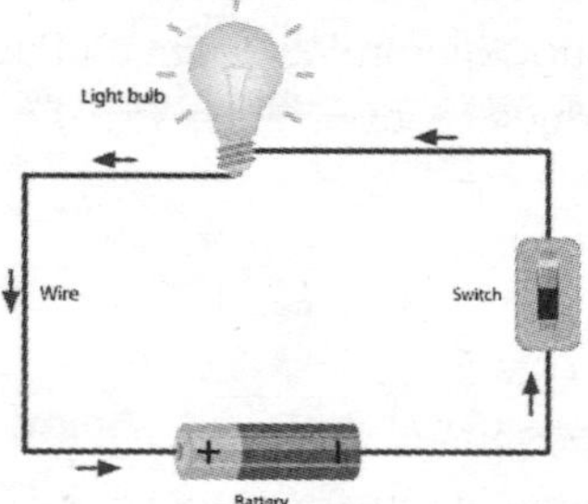

3

Who invented these Industrial Revolution creations? The 'Spinning Jenny', the first practical steam engine, and the Rocket locomotive.

4

Name the world's four tallest buildings, as of January 2018.

5

In which video games franchises would you find Gordon Freeman, Lara Croft, Link, Pikachu and Sephiroth?

6

What are the brand names that have become generic names for the following products? Clear sticky tape, hook-and-loop fastening, plastic storage containers, the raincoat, the vacuum cleaner and the whirlpool bath.

7

Which companies manufactured these best-selling and iconic mobile phone models? The 1100, iPhone, E1100, RAZR, Thunderbolt, K300 and Pearl.

8

Name the architects of the following: Bauhaus School (Dessau), the Duomo (Florence), Piazza San Pietro, Sagrada Familia, Solomon R.Guggenheim Museum, St Paul's Cathedral (London), Sydney Opera House and the White House.

9

Who invented the following? Ball-point pen, dynamite, frozen food, jet engine, microwave oven, safety match, stethoscope, telephone and the World Wide Web.

10

What do the following computing acronyms stand for? ASCII, HTML, HTTP, ISP, PDF, TTS, URL, USB, UX, CPU.

11

Identify these tech companies by their founders. Mark Zuckerberg; Jeff Bezos; Bill Gates and Paul Allen; Fusajiro Yamauchi; Masaru Ibuka and Akio Morita; Sergey Brin and Larry Page; Pierre Morad Omidyar; Thomas J. Watson; Steve Jobs, Steve Wozniak and Ronald Wayne; Lee Byung-chull; Jerry Yang and David Filo.

Answers on page 220

The 2010s

1

In 2011, which African state became the world's youngest country?

2

Which cities hosted the Summer Olympic Games in 2012 and 2016?

3

What were the first three novels in E. L. James's Fifty Shades series?

4

What are the titles of the four studio albums Taylor Swift released between 2010 and 2017?

5

Can you identify these *Time* magazine Persons of the Year from the year and initials? M.Z. (2010), B.O. (2012), P.F. (2013), A.M. (2015), D.T. (2016).

6

Which countries did the following figures lead during the 2010s? Alexis Tsipras, Cristina Fernández de Kirchner, Jacinda Ardern, Justin Trudeau, Nicolás Maduro and Xi Jinping.

7

In which years did the following events take place? Catalonia unilaterally declares independence from Spain; *Charlie Hebdo* shootings in Paris; Deepwater Horizon oil spill; Osama bin Laden is killed; Jorge Mario Bergoglio becomes Pope Francis; the Higgs boson is discovered; the music star Prince dies.

8

Can you identify these eight notable people who died in the decade (initials, dates and professions provided)? N.M. (1918–2013, South African president); L.F. (1922–2011, British artist); M.T. (1925–2013, British political leader); H.H. (1926–2017, American publishing magnate); A.S. (1928–2014, former Israeli prime minister); E.W. (1928–2016, Romanian-born American Holocaust-survivor and writer); W.C. (1939–2015, American horror film director); W.M. (1940–2011, first female African Nobel Peace Prize winner).

9

Who wrote these books? *All the Light We Cannot See*, *The Fault in Our Stars*, *The Ministry of Utmost Happiness*, *Gone Girl*, *Life After Life*, *The Dinner*, *Room*, *The Sense of an Ending* and *A Visit from the Goon Squad*.

10

Who had the ten most followed Twitter accounts in the world at the beginning of 2018?

11

Who had big hits with these albums of the 2010s? *21*, *Born This Way*, *Born to Die*, *Loud*, *Ceremonials*, *Pure Heroine*, *Random Access Memories*, *Sigh No More*, *Take Care*, *Teenage Dream*, *Unorthodox Jukebox* and *Up All Night*.

Answers on page 221

General Knowledge VI

1

What is the only ball sport to have been played on the moon's surface?

2

What is the name of the beagle that stars in Charles M. Schulz's *Peanuts* comic strip, and what is his best friend (a yellow bird) called?

3

What are the three stages of the triple jump known as?

4

Who played Egon Spengler, Louis Tully, Peter Venkman and Ray Stantz in the 1984 blockbuster movie, *Ghostbusters*?

5

In mythology, what are the five rivers of Hades called?

6

Where are the Walt Disney Company's six major park destinations?

7

What are the names of the Seven Hills of Rome?

8

For which international organizations are these the acronyms? EFTA, FAO, IAEA, ICRC, OPEC, UNESCO, WHO, WIPO.

9

What obsessions do the following nine manias relate to? Automania, bibliomania, choreomania, chrematomania, dipsomania, kleptomania, monomania, pyromania and timbromania.

10

Which ten countries have the world's highest capital cities in terms of altitude?

11

In which countries did the following airlines originate? Aeroflot, Aegean Airlines, Aer Lingus, Cathay Pacific, Druk Air, El Al, Etihad Airways, Gulf Air, Iberia, KLM, Lufthansa and Nordica.

Answers on page 222

Answers

General Knowledge I

1 Orchids

2 Noel and Liam Gallagher

3 Berlin, Hamburg and Munich

4 George Washington, Thomas Jefferson, Theodore Roosevelt and Abraham Lincoln

5 Joey Bishop, Sammy Davis Jr, Peter Lawford, Dean Martin and Frank Sinatra

6 Blue, green, orange, red, white and yellow

7 The Colossus of Rhodes, the Great Pyramid at Giza, the Hanging Gardens of Babylon, the Lighthouse at Alexandria, the Mausoleum at Halicarnassus, the statue of Zeus at Olympia and the Temple of Artemis at Ephesus

Hanging Gardens of Babylon

8 Michael Phelps, Paavo Nurmi, Mark Spitz, Carl Lewis, Sawao Kato, Matt Biondi, Usain Bolt and Ray Ewry

9 Dakar, Damascus, Dhaka, Dili, Djibouti, Dodoma, Doha, Dublin and Dushanbe

10 Arkansas, Illinois, Iowa, Kentucky, Louisiana, Minnesota, Mississippi, Missouri, Tennessee and Wisconsin

11 Pharmacist, worker with brass, candle maker, wig maker, barrel maker, fruit and vegetable seller, horse groom, scribe, a dock labourer, curer of animal hides and wagon maker

---

Countries of the World

1 Lesotho

2 The Cook Islands and Niuie

3 Belgium, the Netherlands and Luxembourg

4 Denmark, Djibouti, Dominica and the Dominican Republic

5 Ethiopia, Belize, Sri Lanka, Thailand and Zimbabwe

6 Venezuela, Saudi Arabia, Canada, Iran, Iraq and Kuwait

7 Austria, Croatia, Romania, Serbia, Slovakia, Slovenia and Ukraine

8 Australian Capital Territory, New South Wales, Queensland, South Australia, Tasmania, Victoria, Western Australia and the Northern Territory

9 Finland, Australia, Norway, Netherlands, Denmark, USA, China, New Zealand and France

10 Italy, China, Spain, France, Germany, India, Mexico, the United Kingdom, Russia and the USA

11 Armenia, Azerbaijan, Belarus, Estonia, Georgia, Kazakhstan, Kyrgyzstan, Latvia, Lithuania, Moldova, Russia, Tajikistan, Turkmenistan, Ukraine and Uzbekistan

---

Sport I

1 Pittsburgh Steelers

2 Muhammad Ali and George Foreman

3 Swimming, cycling and running

4 The Masters, the US Open, the Open and the PGA Championship

5 Australia, England, France, New Zealand and South Africa

6 Marseille, AC Milan, Ajax, Juventus, Borussia Dortmund and Real Madrid

7 Goalkeeper, goal defence, wing defence, centre, wing attack, goal attack and goal shooter

8 Argentina, Brazil, England, France, Germany (including as West Germany), Italy, Spain and Uruguay

9 Pitcher, catcher, first baseman, second baseman, third baseman, shortstop, left fielder, center fielder and right fielder

10 Roger Federer, Pete Sampras, Ivan Lendl, Jimmy Connors, Novak Djokovic, John McEnroe, Rafael Nadal, Björn Borg, Andre Agassi and Lleyton Hewitt

11 Austria, Canada, France, Germany, Italy, Japan, Norway, Russia, South Korea, Switzerland, USA and Yugoslavia

---

Cinema I

1 Mumbai

2 Bill and Ted

3 *Blue*, *White* and *Red*

4 Jean-Pierre Jeunet, Giuseppe Tornatore, Ang Lee and Roberto Benigni

5 Chico, Groucho, Gummo, Harpo and Zeppo

6 Sean Connery, Roger Moore, George Lazenby, Timothy Dalton, Pierce Brosnan and Daniel Craig

7 Bashful, Doc, Dopey, Grumpy, Happy, Sleepy and Sneezy

8 Gregory Peck, Marlon Brando, Johnny Depp, Heath Ledger, Mark Hamill, Anthony Perkins, Sylvester Stallone and Brad Pitt

9 *Planet of the Apes*, *Beneath the Planet of the Apes*, *Escape from the Planet of the Apes*, *Conquest of the Planet of the Apes*, *Battle for the Planet of the Apes*, *Planet of the Apes* (remake), *Rise of the Planet of the Apes*, *Dawn of the Planet of the Apes* and *War for the Planet of the Apes*

10 *Chicago*, *The Lion King*, *Funny Girl*, *The Sound of Music*, *Singin' in the Rain*, *Grease*, *Mary Poppins*, *Meet Me in St Louis*, *The Rocky Horror Picture Show* and *Cabaret*

11 *The Muppet Movie*, *The Great Muppet Caper*, *The Muppets Take Manhattan*, *The Muppet Christmas Carol*, *Muppet Classic Theater*, *Muppet Treasure Island*, *Muppets From Space*, *Kermit's Swamp Years*, *It's a Very Merry Muppet Christmas Movie*, *The Muppets' Wizard of Oz*, *The Muppets* and *Muppets Most Wanted*

Kings, Queens and Other Leaders

1 Augustus

2 Kim Jong-il and Kim Jong-un

3 Corsica, Elba and St Helena

4 Mutsuhito, Yoshihito, Hirohito and Akihito

5 Victoria, Haile Selassie, Louis XVI, Alexander the Great and Nicholas II

6 Martha Washington, Eleanor Roosevelt, Jacqueline Kennedy, Pat Nixon, Betty Ford and Barbara Bush

7 Zachary Taylor, Abraham Lincoln, James A. Garfield, William McKinley, Warren G. Harding, Franklin D. Roosevelt and John F. Kennedy

8 Trygve Lie, Dag Hammarskjöld, U Thant, Kurt Waldheim, Javier Pérez de Cuéllar, Boutros Boutros-Ghali, Kofi Annan and Ban Ki-moon

9 Vladimir Lenin, Josef Stalin, Georgy Malenkov, Nikita Khrushchev, Leonid Brezhnev, Yuri Andropov, Konstantin Chernenko, Mikhail Gorbachev and Gennady Yanayev

10 Ptolomaic, Saxe-Coburg and Gotha, Habsburg, Romanov, Tudor, Carolingian, Bourbon, David, Savoy and Qing

11 Alben W. Barkley, Richard Nixon, Lyndon B. Johnson, Hubert Humphrey, Spiro Agnew, Gerald Ford, Nelson A. Rockefeller, Walter Mondale, George H. W. Bush, Dan Quayle, Al Gore, Dick Cheney, Joe Biden and Mike Pence

---

Land Animals

1 Four

2 Dromedary and Bactrian camel

3 Cheetah, pronghorn and springbok

4 African elephant, Asian elephant, white rhinoceros and giraffe

5 Bonobos, chimpanzees, gorillas, humans and orangutans

6 Snow leopard, cougar, jaguar, leopard, lion and tiger

7 Buck, jack, billy, stallion, cob, drake and ewe

8 North American black bear, Asiatic black bear, brown (including Grizzly) bears, giant panda, polar bear, sloth bear, spectacled (Andean) bear and sun bear

9 Cow, doe, jenny, jill, vixen, nanny, pen, ewe and mare

10 Fawn, nymph, elver, kid, gosling, leveret, joey, spat, spiderling and cygnet

11 Orangutan, cow, domestic dog, goat, zebra, African elephant, red kangaroo, sheep, chimpanzee, lion, domestic pig and red fox

---

Literature I

1 *The Metamorphosis*

2 Sherlock Holmes and Dr Watson

3 Alexei, Dmitri and Ivan

4 Genesis, Exodus, Leviticus and Numbers

5 Norway, Russia, Turkey, South Africa and the Czech Republic (formerly Czechoslovakia)

6 *Prince Caspian*, *The Voyage of the Dawn Treader*, *The Silver Chair*, *The Horse and His Boy*, *The Magician's Nephew* and *The Last Battle*

7 *The Philosopher's Stone*, *The Chamber of Secrets*, *The Prisoner of Azkaban*, *The Goblet of Fire*, *The Order of the Phoenix*, *The Half-Blood Prince* and *The Deathly Hallows*

8 Noun, pronoun, verb, adjective, adverb, preposition, conjunction and interjection

9 Frodo Baggins, Samwise 'Sam' Gamgee, Gandalf the Grey, Legolas, Gimli, Aragorn (Strider), Boromir, Meriadoc 'Merry' Brandybuck and Peregrin 'Pippin' Took

10 Alice Munro, Jean-Paul Sartre, Toni Morrison, Thomas Mann, Doris Lessing, Rudyard Kipling, Aleksandr Solzshenitsyn, Henryk Sienkiewicz, Mo Yan and Octavio Paz

11 *A Midsummer Night's Dream*; *All's Well That Ends Well*; *Antony and Cleopatra*; *As You Like It*; *The Comedy of Errors*; *Coriolanus*; *Cymbeline*; *Hamlet*; *Henry IV, Part 1*; *Henry IV, Part 2*; *Henry V*; *Henry VI, Part 1*; *Henry VI, Part 2*; *Henry VI, Part 3*; *Henry VIII*; *Julius Caesar*; *King John*; *King Lear*; *Love's Labour's Lost*; *Macbeth*; *Measure for Measure*; *The Merchant of Venice*; *The Merry Wives of Windsor*; *Much Ado About Nothing*; *Othello*; *Richard II*; *Richard III*; *Romeo and Juliet*; *The Taming of the Shrew*; *The Tempest*; *Timon of Athens*; *Titus Andronicus*; *Troilus and Cressida*; *Twelfth Night*; *Two Gentlemen of Verona*; *The Winter's Tale*

The 1940s

1 London

2 Hiroshima and Nagasaki

3 Winston Churchill, Franklin D. Roosevelt and Joseph Stalin

4 Bill Kenny, Deek Watson, Charlie Fuqua and Hoppy Jones

5 1944, 1941, 1940, 1949 and 1948

6 Lucille Ball, Laurence Olivier, Betty Grable, Lauren Bacall, Princess Elizabeth (later Queen Elizabeth II) and Rita Hayworth

7 *Road to Singapore*, *Road to Zanzibar*, *Road to Morocco*, *Road to Utopia*, *Road to Rio*, *Road to Bali* and *The Road to Hong Kong*

8 Nikola Tesla, Max Planck, Paul Klee, Benito Mussolini, John Maynard Keynes, Sergei Eisenstein, Lou Gehrig, Carole Lombard

9 Jorge Luis Borges, Benjamin Spock, Anne Frank, Winston Churchill, Primo Levi, Joseph Schumpeter, Eugene O'Neill, Simone de Beauvoir and Albert Camus

10 *Rebecca*, *How Green was My Valley*, *Mrs Miniver*, *Casablanca*, *Going My Way*, *The Lost Weekend*, *The Best Years of Our Lives*, *Gentleman's Agreement*, *Hamlet* and *All the King's Men*

11 Burma, Italy, France, Israel, Spain, Cuba, Brazil, Vietnam, Pakistan, New Zealand, Iran and Australia

---

Games and Pastimes

1 23

2 Bobby Fischer and Boris Spassky

3 Florida Avenue, Park Place and Boardwalk

4 Clubs, diamonds, hearts and spades

5 Karate, judo, jujitsu, aikido and kendo

6 Bishop, king, knight, pawn, queen and rook

7 F, H, V, W, Y; and Q and Z

8 Black, blue, brown, green, pink, red, white and yellow

9 Billiard room, conservatory, dining room, hall, kitchen, library, lounge and study

10 High card, one pair, two pair, three of a kind, straight, flush, full house, four of a kind, straight flush and royal flush

Royal Flush

Straight Flush

Four of a Kind

Full House

Flush

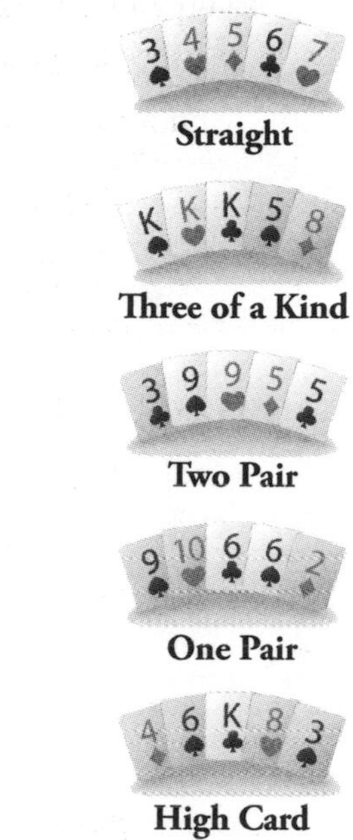

Straight

Three of a Kind

Two Pair

One Pair

High Card

11 Suspects: Reverend Green, Colonel Mustard, Mrs Peacock, Professor Plum, Miss Scarlett and Mrs White. Weapons: candlestick, dagger, lead pipe, revolver, rope and spanner

---

Science I

1 The double-helix structure of DNA

2 Hydrogen and oxygen

3 Igneous, metamorphic and sedimentary

4 Left atrium, right atrium, left ventricle and right ventricle

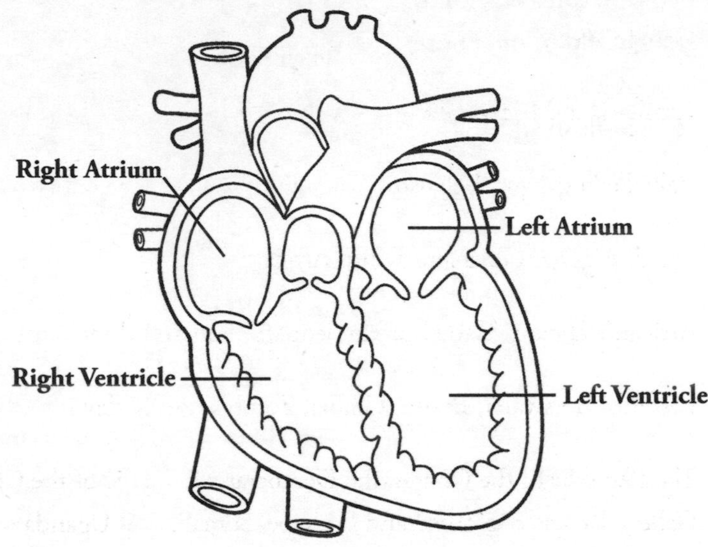

5 Ceres, Eris, Haumea, Makemake and Pluto

6 Cesium, francium, lithium, potassium, rubidium and sodium

7 Ampere, candela, kelvin, kilogram, metre, mole and second

8 Domain, kingdom, phylum, class, order, family, genus and species

9 1, 10, 11, 100, 101, 1010, 11001, 110010 and 1100100

10 Health of new-born baby, wind speed, sea swell and wave height, force of tornadoes, impaired consciousness, personal sexual history, mineral hardness, acidity/alkalinity of a solution, seismic energy released in earthquake and chili heat

11 Argon, chlorine, fluorine, helium, hydrogen, krypton, neon, nitrogen, oxygen, radon and xenon

Africa

1 George Weah

2 Kinshasa and Brazzaville

3 Italy, Portugal and Belgium

4 Chad, Algeria, Libya and South Africa

5 African elephant, Cape buffalo, leopard, lion and rhinoceros

6 Lesotho, Botswana, Benin, Ghana, Zambia and Malawi

7 The Republic of the Congo, the Democratic Republic of the Congo, Gabon, Kenya, São Tomé and Principe, Somalia and Uganda

8 Nadine Gordimer, Naguib Mahfouz, Thomas Mofolo, J. M. Coetzee, Ben Okri, Tsitsi Dangarembga, Chinua Achebe and Wole Soyinka

9 The Seychelles, Mauritius, Morocco, Tunisia, Namibia, Kenya, Botswana, Egypt and South Africa

10 Ethiopia, Malawi, Uganda, Central African Republic, Kenya, Zambia, Ghana, Zaire, South Africa and Gabon

11 Luanda, Gaborone, Ouagadougou, Cairo, Addis Ababa, Nairobi, Monrovia, Antananarivo, Rabat, Windhoek, Abuja, Kigali, Freetown, Khartoum and Lusaka

Transport

1 1860s

2 Orville and Wilbur

3 Bow, fathom and knot

4 Ford, Rolls-Royce, Lotus and Volkswagen

5 Golden Gate Bridge, Pont d'Avignon, Ponte Vecchio, the Öresund Bridge and Howrah Bridge

6 Madrid train station, Maputo, Mumbai, Paris, Istanbul and Edinburgh

7 The Soviet Union, the USA, France, Japan, China, the UK and India

8 De Lorean, General Lee (Dodge Charger), Aston Martin DB5, Ford Anglia, KITT (Pontiac Trans Am), The FAB 1 (Rolls-Royce), Ford Gran Torino and GMC G-series van

9 Australia, Portugal, Hungary, Brazil, the USA, France, Italy, the UK and Belgium

10 Stockholm (Arlanda), Buenos Aires Airport, New York (John F. Kennedy International), Los Angeles International, London (Heathrow), Lagos (Murtala Muhammed), Tokyo (Narita), Shanghai Hongqiao International Airport, Sydney Airport and Berlin (Tegel 'Otto Lilienthal')

11 Romania, the USA, South Korea, Italy, France, Sweden, China, Spain, Czechoslovakia, India, Japan and Germany

Music I

1 Marilyn Monroe

2 Wolfgang Amadeus Mozart and Antonio Salieri

3 José Carreras, Plácido Domingo and Luciano Pavarotti

4 Micky Dolenz, Davy Jones, Michael Nesmith and Peter Tork

5 Baby, Ginger, Posh, Scary and Sporty

6 Soprano, mezzo-soprano, contralto, countertenor, tenor and baritone

7 'Beat It', 'Billie Jean', 'Human Nature', 'PYT (Pretty Young Thing'), 'The Girl Is Mine', 'Thriller' and 'Wanna Be Startin' Somethin'

8 Satchmo, Duke Ellington, Count Basie, Dizzy Gillespie, Lady Day, Cannonbal Adderley, Fats Waller and Bird

9 Blitzen, Comet, Cupid, Dasher, Dancer, Donner, Prancer, Rudolph and Vixen

10 Wolfgang Amadeus Mozart, Ludwig van Beethoven, Gioachino Rossini, Giuseppe Verdi, Georges Bizet, Richard Wagner, Pyotr Ilyich Tchaikovsky, Giacomo Puccini, Benjamin Britten and John Adams

11 Bono, Elton John, Stevie Wonder, David Bowie, Freddie Mercury, George Michael, Sting, Tina Turner, Bob Dylan, Marilyn Manson, Gene Simmons, Iggy Pop, Flea, Meat Loaf, Sid Vicious and Slash

---

General Knowledge II

1 Denmark

2 Madeira and the Azores

3 Judaism, Christianity and Islam

4 Gryffindor, Hufflepuff, Ravenclaw and Slytherin

5 Homer, Marge, Bart, Lisa and Maggie

6 Acute, equilateral, isosceles, obtuse, right-angled and scalene

7 Belize, Costa Rica, El Salvador, Guatemala, Honduras, Nicaragua and Panama (see map, right)

8 George Harrison, John Lennon, Paul McCartney, Ringo Starr, John Deacon, Brian May, Freddie Mercury and Roger Taylor

9 Denmark, Estonia, Finland, Germany, Latvia, Lithuania, Poland, Russia and Sweden

10 Chad, Cuba, Fiji, Iran, Iraq, Laos, Mali, Oman, Peru and Togo

11 A partridge in a pear tree, two turtle doves, three French hens, four calling birds, five gold rings, six geese a-laying, seven swans a-swimming, eight maids a-milking, nine ladies dancing, ten lords a-leaping, eleven pipers piping and twelve drummers drumming

---

History I

1 Vasco de Gama

2 Bonn and East Berlin

3 *Niña*, *Pinta* and *Santa Maria*

4 Abraham Lincoln, James A. Garfield, William McKinley and John F. Kennedy

5 Augustus, Tiberius, Caligula, Claudius and Nero

6 Catherine of Aragon, Anne Boleyn, Jane Seymour, Anne of Cleves, Catherine Howard and Catherine Parr

7 George W. Bush, Abraham Lincoln, Dwight D. Eisenhower, Angela Merkel, Margaret Thatcher, Napoleon and Richard Nixon

8 Laika, Usain Bolt, Benazir Bhutto, Pheidippides, Roger Bannister, Robin Knox-Johnston, Dr Christiaan Barnard and Roald Amundsen

9 Actium, Hastings, Antioch, Agincourt, Austerlitz, Gettysburg, Passchendaele and Monte Cassino, Tet Offensive.

10 2001, 1492, 1991, 1865, 1918, 1949, 1994, 1947, 1215 and 1776

11 Simón Bolívar, Christopher Columbus, Jesus Christ ('The Saviour'), George III of England, James Monroe, William Pitt the Elder, Louis XV of France, Marthinus Pretoria, Athena, Thomas Townshend (Lord Sydney), Elizabeth I of England (the Virgin Queen) and George Washington

Geography I

1 Hungary

2 Paris and Constantinople (now Istanbul)

3 Kangchenjunga, Lhotse and Makalu

4 Vanuatu, Vatican City, Venezuela and Vietnam

5 Cuba, Haiti, Dominican Republic, Jamaica, and Trinidad and Tobago

6 Nile, Yangtze, Missouri, Amazon, Murray and Volga

7 Angel Falls, Venezuela; Tugela Falls, South Africa; Cataratas Las Tres Hermanas, Peru; Olo'upena Falls, USA; Catarata Yumbilla, Peru; Vinnufossen and Balaifossen both in Norway.

8 Caspian Sea, Lake Superior, Lake Victoria, Lake Huron, Lake Michigan, Tanganyika, Baikal and Great Bear Lake

9 Athens (Greece), Toronto (Canada), Rome (Italy), Istanbul (Turkey), Budapest (Hungary), Moscow (Russia), Luxor (Egypt), Hong Kong and Dubai

10 Malta, the Maldives, Saint Kitts and Nevis, Marshall Islands, Liechtenstein, San Marino, Tuvalu, Nauru, Monaco and the Vatican City

11 Real, Yuan Renminbi, Koruna, Forint, Shekel, Yen, Ringgit, Dirham, Zloty, Ruble, Bolivar and Dong

The 1950s

1 Rosa Parks

2 Helsinki and Melbourne

3 Joy (Jocelyn), Teddie (Hazel) and Babs (Babette)

4 1955, 1957, 1953 and 1951

5 Konrad Adenauer, John Foster Dulles, Nikita Khrushchev, Charles de Gaulle and Dwight D. Eisenhower

6 Belgium, France, Italy, Luxembourg, the Netherlands and West Germany

7 Ronald Reagan, Brigitte Bardot, John F. Kennedy, Audrey Hepburn, Marilyn Monroe, Grace Kelly and Natalie Wood

8 William Randolph Hearst, Frank Lloyd Wright, Joseph Stalin, Diego Rivera, Imre Nagy, George Orwell, Alan Turing and Eva Perón

9 Albert Einstein, Claude Lévi-Strauss, Boris Pasternak, Ray Bradbury, Isaac Asimov, Thor Heyerdahl, Vladimir Nabokov, Czesław Miłosz and Jack Kerouac

10 *All About Eve*, *An American in Paris*, *The Greatest Show on Earth*, *From Here to Eternity*, *On the Waterfront*, *Marty*, *Around the World in 80 Days*, *The Bridge on the River Kwai*, *Gigi* and *Ben-Hur*

11 Mexico, Italy, Ireland, Iraq, Yugoslavia, Libya, West Germany, Canada, Soviet Union, Australia, Sweden and Finland

Famous People I

1 Tutankhamun

2 Nicole Brown Simpson and Ronald Goldman

3 Julius Caesar, Marcus Licinius Crassus and Pompey the Great

4 Matthew, Mark, Luke and John

5 Jackie, Jermaine, Marlon, Michael and Tito

6 Valentina Tereshkova, Svetlana Savitskaya, Sally Ride, Judith Resnik, Kathryn D. Sullivan and Anna Lee Fisher

7 Nefertiti, Louis XVI, Percy Byshe Shelley, John Smith, Emperor Shah Jahan, Elizabeth Barrett Browning and Edward, Duke of Windsor (formerly Edward VIII).

8 Carlsberg, HSBC (Hongkong and Shanghai Banking Corporation), Mitsubishi, Avon Products, The Coca-Cola Company, General Electric, Adidas and Virgin Records

9 John Tyler, Millard Fillmore, Andrew Johnson, Chester Arthur, Theodore Roosevelt, Calvin Coolidge, Harry Truman, Lyndon Johnson and Gerald Ford

10 James Cook, Hernán Cortés, Admiral Zheng He, Amerigo Vespucci, Marco Polo, Abel Tasman, Christopher Columbus, Sir Walter Raleigh, Ferdinand Magellan and David Livingstone

11 Fred Astaire, Marilyn Monroe, Judy Garland, Whoopi Goldberg, Woody Allen, Harry Houdini, John Wayne, Pelé, Voltaire, Julie Andrews, Charlie Sheen, Nicolas Cage, Audrey Hepburn, Sophia Loren and Molière

---

The Arts I

1 *Mona Lisa*

2 Plato and Aristotle

3 Seventeenth century, nineteenth century and sixteenth century

4 *La Gioconda*, *Rigoletto*, *The Turn of the Screw* and *Tosca*

5 Grant Wood, Jan van Eyck, Pierre-Auguste Renoir, Pablo Picasso and Rembrandt

6 Pyotr Ilyich Tchaikovsky, Adolphe Adam, Sergei Prokofiev, Igor Stravinsky, Ludwig Minkus and Felix Mendelssohn (his music was used posthumously)

7 Museum of Modern Art, New York; Uffizi Gallery, Florence; Trinity College, Dublin; Museo del Prado, Madrid; The Sistine Chapel, Vatican City; the Convent of Santa Maria delle Grazie, Milan; the Louvre, Paris (see picture opposite)

8 Michelangelo, Margaret Keane, Frida Kahlo, Johannes Vermeer, Vincent van Gogh, Joseph Mallord William Turner, Christy Brown and Séraphine Louis

9 Calliope, Clio, Erato, Euterpe, Melpomene, Polyhymnia, Terpsichore, Thalia and Urania

10 China, Norway, Mexico, Austria, USA, Italy, the Netherlands, Belgium, Spain and Russia

11 *Thespis*, *Trial by Jury*, *The Sorcerer*, *HMS Pinafore*, *The Pirates of Penzance*, *Patience*, *Iolanthe*, *Princess Ida*, *The Mikado*, *Ruddigore*, *The Yeoman of the Guard*, *The Gondoliers*, *Utopia Ltd* and *The Grand Duke*

Up in the Sky

1 Bald eagle

2 The UK and France

3 Wandering albatross, great white pelican and Marabou stork

4 Cumulus, stratus, cirrus and nimbus

5 Troposphere, stratosphere, mesosphere, thermosphere and exosphere

6 Cassowaries, elephant birds, emus, kiwis, moa and rheas

7 Blue, green, indigo, orange, red, violet and yellow

8 Baron Manfred Von Richthofen, John Glenn, Amelia Earhart, Howard Hughes, Steve Fossett, Joseph-Michel and Jacques-Étienne Montgolfier, Charles Lindbergh, and Paul Tibbets

9 Ocean of Storms, Sea of Cold, Sea of Showers or Sea of Rains, Sea of Fertility, Sea of Tranquility, Sea of Clouds, Sea of Serenity, Southern Sea and Sea of Islands

10 Sirius, Canopus, Alpha Centauri (Rigil Kentaurus), Arcturus, Vega, Capella, Rigel, Procyon, Achernar and Betelgeuse

11 Roald Amundsen, Subhas Chandra Bose, Amy Johnson, Dag Hammarskjöld, Rocky Marciano, Buddy Holly, Otis Redding, Steve Fossett, Lech Kaczynski, Stevie Ray Vaughan, Hansie Cronje and Aaliyah

---

Food and Drink I

1 Pastel de nata

2 A turkey and a chicken

3 South Australia, New South Wales and Victoria

4 Germany, France, Hungary, Italy

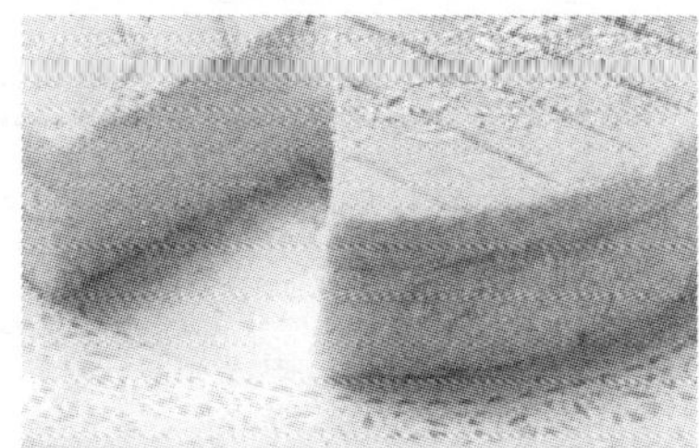

5 Tomato, mozzarella, basil, salt and olive oil

6 Potato, lentils, cauliflower, chicken, cheese and spinach

7 Indonesia, USA, China, Jamaica, UK, France and Japan

8 Nigeria, Côte d'Ivoire, Brazil, Turkey, Spain, Iran, USA and China

9 Lasagne doughnuts, vodka martini, Earl Grey tea, lollipops, marmalade sandwiches, spinach, pizza and honey

10 Bloody Mary, Singapore Sling, Long Island Ice Tea, Mojito, Margarita, Cosmopolitan, Harvey Wallbanger, Screwdriver, White Russian and Manhattan

11 Japan, Brazil, Denmark, South Africa, Argentina, Thailand, Belgium, USA, China, the Netherlands, India, Mexico, Canada, Italy, Czech Republic, Australia and Poland

Politics

1 Monica Lewinsky

2 Muhammad Ali Jinnah and Jawaharlal Nehru

3 Legislative, executive and judicial branches

4 The International Criminal Court, the International Monetary Fund, the North Atlantic Treaty Organization and the Organisation for Economic Co-operation and Development

5 China, France, Russia, UK and USA

6 Arabic, Chinese, English, French, Russian and Spanish

7 Canada, France, Germany, Italy, Japan, UK and USA

8 Albania, Bulgaria, Czechoslovakia, East Germany, Hungary, Poland, Romania and the Soviet Union

9 Paris, Florence, Granada, Vienna, St Petersburg, Beijing, Istanbul, Jaipur and Edinburgh

10 Iceland, Germany, Republic of Ireland, UK, Israel, India, Vatican City, Sweden, Poland and Russia

11 Austria, Belgium, Bulgaria, Croatia, Cyprus, Czech Republic, Denmark, Estonia, Finland, France, Germany, Greece, Hungary, Ireland, Italy, Latvia, Lithuania, Luxembourg, Malta, Netherlands, Poland, Portugal, Romania, Slovakia, Slovenia, Spain and Sweden

---

Asia

1 Sachin Tendulkar

2 The Yangtze and the Yellow River

3 Agra, Delhi and Jaipur

4 Hokkaido, Honshu, Kyushu and Shikoku

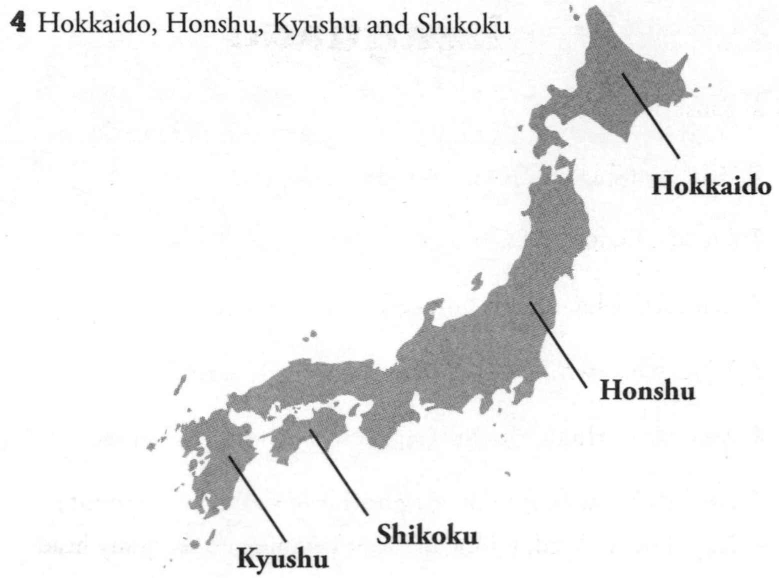

5 Lu Xun, Rohinton Mistry, Arundhati Roy, Jung Chang and Haruki Murakami

6 Bhutan, Iraq, Kyrgyzstan, North Korea, Singapore and Yemen

7 Rajasthan, Madhya Pradesh, Maharashtra, Uttar Pradesh, Jammu and Kashmir, Gujarat and Karnataka

8 Cambodia, Indonesia, Japan, the Philippines, Singapore, India, South Korea and Hong Kong (China)

9 China, Japan, Jordan, India, Kazakhstan, Cambodia, Turkmenistan, Indonesia and Myanmar (Burma)

10 Baku, Dhaka, Thimphu, Phnom Penh, Vientiane, Ulaanbaatar, Naypyidaw, Kathmandu, Manila and Hanoi

11 Municipalities: Beijing, Chongqing, Shanghai and Tianjin; autonomous regions: Guangxi, Inner Mongolia, Ningxia, Tibet and Xinjiang; special administrative regions: Hong Kong and Macau

Language

1 Sanskrit

2 Britain and USA

3 French, Dutch and German

4 Gamma, delta, epsilon and zeta

5 Who, what, where, when and why

6 Mandarin, Hindi, Bengali, Japanese, Arabic and Javanese

7 As a matter of fact; I know, right; I love you; in my opinion; laughing out loud; rolling on floor laughing; shaking my head

8 Bolognese, Cantabrigian, Capetonian, Florentine, Saigonese, Las Vegan, Muscovite and Neapolitan

9 Angola, Brazil, Cape Verde, East Timor, Equatorial Guinea, Guinea-Bissau, Mozambique, Portugal and São Tomé and Príncipe

10 QWERTYUIOP

11 Charlie, delta, echo, foxtrot, golf, hotel, india, juliett, kilo, lima, mike, november, oscar, papa, quebec, romeo, sierra, tango, uniform, victor, whiskey, xray, yankee and zulu

Alpha	Bravo	Charlie	Delta	Echo	Foxtrot
Golf	Hotel	India	Juliet	Kilo	Lima
Mike	November	Oscar	Papa	Quebec	Romeo
Sierra	Tango	Uniform	Victor	Whiskey	X-ray
Yankee	Zulu				

The 1960s

1 Checkpoint Charlie

2 Roy Lichtenstein and Andy Warhol

3 Rome, Tokyo and Mexico City

4 John F. Kennedy, Martin Luther King Jr, Lyndon B. Johnson and William Westmoreland

5 Scooby-Doo, Fred Jones, Daphne Blake, Velma Dinkley and Norville 'Shaggy' Rogers

6 Richard Burton, Judy Garland, Frank Sinatra, Elvis Presley, Roman Polanski and John Lennon

7 1961, 1969, 1963, 1967, 1962, 1965 and 1968

8 David Gilmour, Nick Mason, Richard Wright, Roger Waters, Syd Barrett; Jimi Hendrix, Mitch Mitchell and Noel Redding

9 Michel Foucault, John Fowles, Saul Bellow, Gabriel García Márquez, Muriel Spark, Mikhail Bulgakov, Kurt Vonnegut, Günter Grass and Jean Rhys

10 *The Apartment*, *West Side Story*, *Lawrence of Arabia*, *Tom Jones*, *My Fair Lady*, *The Sound of Music*, *A Man for All Seasons*, *In the Heat of the Night*, *Oliver!* and *Midnight Cowboy*

11 Italy, Czechoslovakia, Chile, Egypt, Australia, The Netherlands, Tanzania, Soviet Union, Canada, Democratic Republic of the Congo, Indonesia and East Germany

---

Music II

1 Nikolai Rimsky-Korsakov

2 Neneh Cherry and Youssou N'Dour

3 Violin, guitar and drums

4 Benny Andersson, Agnetha Fältskog, Anni-Frid Lyngstad and Björn Ulvaeus

5 Niall Horan, Liam Payne, Harry Styles, Louis Tomlinson and Zayn Malik

6 Construction worker, cowboy, GI, leatherman, Native American and policeman

7 *Titanic*, *Rocky III*, *The Graduate*, *Butch Cassidy and the Sundance Kid*, *Frozen*, *Saturday Night Fever* and *Top Gun*

8 Bart Howard, Hoagy Carmichael, Duke Ellington, Henry Mancini, John Kander, Cole Porter, George Gershwin and Irving Berlin

9 Ireland, India, Japan, Belgium, France, China, Bhutan, Denmark and the Netherlands

10 Johann Sebastian Bach, Carl Orff, Jean Sibelius, Antonio Vivaldi, Johannes Brahms, George Frideric Handel, Ludwig van Beethoven, Gustav Holst, Edvard Grieg and Edward Elgar

11 Studio albums: *Madonna*, *Like a Virgin*, *True Blue*, *Like a Prayer*, *Erotica*, *Bedtime Stories*, *Ray of Light*, *Music*, *American Life*, *Confessions on a Dance Floor*, *Hard Candy*, *MDNA* and *Rebel Heart*. Soundtracks: *Who's That Girl*, *I'm Breathless* and *Evita*

General Knowledge III

1 1997

2 Statler and Waldorf

3 Huey, Dewey and Louie

4 Sanguine, choleric, melancholic and phlegmatic

5 Red, green, yellow, white and blue

6 Germany, Austria, Liechtenstein, Belgium, Luxembourg and Switzerland (see map opposite)

7 Baptism, confirmation, Eucharist, penance/reconciliation, anointing of the sick, holy orders and marriage

8 Ganymede, Titan, Callisto, Io, the Moon, Europa, Triton and Titania

9 Cousin Itt, Grandmama (aka Eudora Addams), Lurch, Master Gomez Addams, Morticia Addams, Pugsley Uno Addams, Thing, Uncle Fester and Wednesday Friday Addams

10 Johan Cruyff Arena, Camp Nou, Allianz Arena, Goodison Park, Ibrox, San Siro, Old Trafford, Parc des Princes, Estádio do Dragão and the Santiago Bernabéu Stadium

11 Mikhail Botvinnik, Vasily Smyslov, Mikhail Tal, Tigran Petrosian, Boris Spassky, Bobby Fischer, Anatoly Karpov, Garry Kasparov, Alexander Khalifman, Viswanathan Anand, Ruslan Ponomariov, Rustam Kasimdzhanov, Veselin Topalov, Vladimir Kramnik and Magnus Carlsen

Heroes

1 Jim Lee

2 Alan Moore and Dave Gibbons

3 Blossom, Bubbles and Buttercup

4 The Human Torch, the Invisible Woman, Mister Fantastic and The Thing

5 Snowy, Professor Calculus, Captain Haddock, and Thomson and Thompson

6 Jason Lee Scott, Kimberly Hart, Zack Taylor, Trini Kwan, Billy Cranston and Zordon

7 Aquaman, Batman, The Flash, Green Lantern, Martian Manhunter, Superman and Wonder Woman

8 Donatello, Leonardo, Michelangelo, Raphael, Splinter, April O'Neil, Casey Jones and The Shredder

9 Coil Man, Fluid Man and Multi-Man; Namor, Doctor Strange and the Hulk; Batman, Superman and Wonder Woman

10 Storm, Nightcrawler, Beast, Wolverine, Mystique, Cyclops, Magneto, Rogue, Professor X and Havok

11 Batman, Captain America, Catwoman, Iceman, The Green Hornet, The Hulk, Iron Man, Magneto, Mr Fantastic, Robin, Spider-Man, Supergirl, Superman, The Thing and Wonder Woman

Europe

1 Andorra

2 Petrograd and Leningrad

3 Corinthian, Doric and Ionic

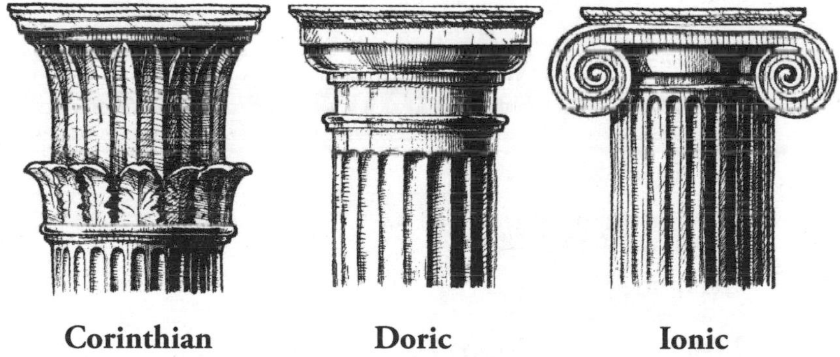

Corinthian **Doric** **Ionic**

4 Belgrade, Budapest, Bratislava and Vienna

5 Denmark, Finland, Iceland, Norway and Sweden

6 Bulgaria, Georgia, Romania, Russia, Turkey and Ukraine

7 Munich, Rome, Paris, Madrid, Amsterdam, Florence and London

8 Bosnia and Herzegovina, Croatia, Macedonia, Montenegro, Serbia, Slovenia and Kosovo, which declared independence from Serbia in 2008, although Serbia disputes the claim. The autonomous province is Vojvodina

9 Austria, Belgium, Czech Republic, Denmark, France, Luxembourg, the Netherlands, Poland and Switzerland

10 Tirana, Sofia, Zagreb, Reykjavik, Riga, Valletta, Oslo, Bucharest, Ljubljana and Ankara

11 Baden-Württemberg, Bavaria, Berlin, Brandenburg, Bremen, Hamburg, Hesse, Lower Saxony, Mecklenburg-West Pomerania, North Rhine-Westphalia, Rhineland-Palatinate, Saarland, Saxony, Saxony-Anhalt, Schleswig-Holstein and Thuringia

---

Cinema II

1 *The Jazz Singer*

2 Buzz Lightyear and Woody

3 *The Virgin Spring*, *Through a Glass Darkly* and *Fanny and Alexander*

4 Sonny, Fredo, Michael and Connie

5 China, India, Japan, Nigeria and USA

6 Jacques Rozier, Alain Resnais, François Truffaut, Claude Chabrol, Jacques Demy and Jean-Luc Godard

7 Charles Bronson, Yul Brynner, Horst Buchholz, James Coburn, Brad Dexter, Steve McQueen and Robert Vaughn

8 *Star Wars* (later retitled *Star Wars: Episode IV – A New Hope*), *The Empire Strikes Back*, *Return of the Jedi*, *The Phantom Menace*, *Attack of the Clones*, *Revenge of the Sith*, *The Force Awakens* and *The Last Jedi*

9 Michael Haneke, Laurent Cantet, Lars von Trier, Chen Kaige, Wim Wenders, Roman Polanski, Jane Campion, Carol Reed and Terrence Malick

10 *Fargo*, *Jurassic Park*, *Psycho*, *Jaws*, *La La Land*, *Edward Scissorhands*, *Alien*, *Catch Me If You Can*, *Singin' in the Rain* and *Ghostbusters*

11 *Iron Man*, *The Incredible Hulk*, *Iron Man 2*, *Thor*, *Captain America: The First Avenger*, *The Avengers*, *Iron Man 3*, *Thor: The Dark World*, *Captain America: The Winter Soldier*, *Guardians of the Galaxy*, *Avengers: Age of Ultron*, *Ant-Man*, *Captan America: Civil War*, *Doctor Strange*, *Guardians of the Galaxy Vol. 2*, *Spider-Man: Homecoming*, *Thor: Ragnarok*, *Black Panther*, *Avengers: Infinity War*

Prizes and Awards

1 Malala Yousafzai

2 *The Sound of Music* and *Fiorello!*

3 *It Happened One Night*, *One Flew Over the Cuckoo's Nest* and *The Silence of the Lambs*

4 John Bardeen, Marie Curie, Linus Pauling and Frederick Sanger

5 Madonna, Lady Gaga, Peter Gabriel, R.E.M. and Eminem

6 Chemistry, Economic Sciences, Literature, Peace, Physics and Physiology of Medicine

7 Edith Wharton, Margaret Mitchell, Harper Lee, John Updike, Toni Morrison, E. Annie Proulx and Donna Tartt

8 Lance Armstrong, Usain Bolt, Novak Djokovic, Roger Federer, Rafael Nadal, Michael Schumacher, Sebastian Vettel and Tiger Woods

9 Daniel Day-Lewis, Dustin Hoffman, Fredric March, Gary Cooper, Jack Nicholson, Marlon Brando, Sean Penn, Spencer Tracy and Tom Hanks

10 Beyoncé, Pierre Boulez, Chick Corea, Vladimir Horowitz, Quincy Jones, Alison Krauss, Georg Solti, U2, John Williams and Stevie Wonder

11 Cricket, yacht racing, motor racing, baseball, women's tennis, soccer, rugby league, basketball, golf, ice hockey, badminton, American football, rugby union, horse racing and cycling

---

The Olympics

1 High jump

2 Tommie Smith and John Carlos

3 1916, 1940 and 1944

4 Backstroke, breaststroke, butterfly and freestyle

5 Black, blue, yellow, green and red

6 Floor exercise, pommel horse, still rings, vault, parallel bars and horizontal bars

7 Norway, USA, Germany, USSR, Canada, Austria and Finland

8 Discus, hammer, high jump, javelin, long jump, pole vault, shot put and triple jump

9 USA, USSR, Great Britain, France, Germany, Italy, China, Australia and Sweden

10 100m, long jump, shot put, high jump, 400m, 110m hurdles, discus, pole vault, javelin and 1500m

11 Athens, Paris, St Louis, London, Stockholm, Antwerp, Paris, Amsterdam, Los Angeles and Berlin

The 1970s

1 Ping-pong diplomacy

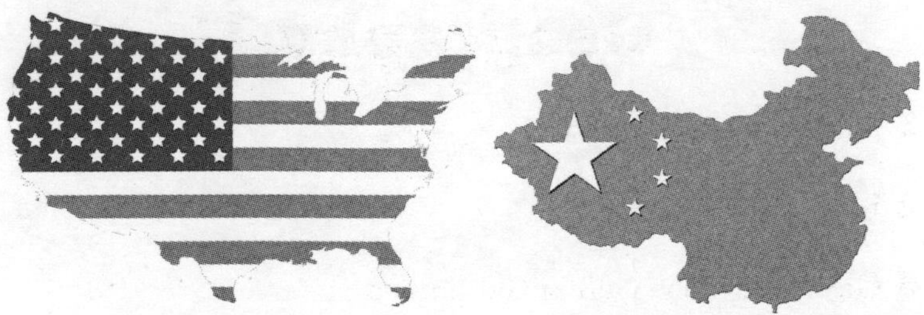

2 Munich and Montreal

3 Keith Emerson, Greg Lake and Carl Palmer

4 Jiang Qing, Wang Hongwen, Yao Wenyuan and Zhang Chunqiao

5 Isabel Perón, Elisabeth Domitien, Indira Gandhi, Golda Meir and Margaret Thatcher

6 Angola, Poland, France, Mexico, Ethiopia and Pakistan

7 Willy Brandt, Richard Nixon, Henry Kissinger, John Sirica, Jimmy Carter, Anwar Sadat and Deng Xiaoping

8 Pablo Picasso, Coco Chanel, Ezra Pound, Charlie Chaplin, Agatha Christie, Kurt Gödel, Jimmy Hoffa and Janis Joplin

9 Wole Soyinka, Frederick Forsyth, Thomas Pynchon, Italo Calvino, Edward Said, Primo Levi, Alex Haley, Milan Kundera and John Le Carré

10 *Patton*, *The French Connection*, *The Godfather*, *The Sting*, *The Godfather Part II*, *One Flew Over the Cuckoo's Nest*, *Rocky*, *Annie Hall*, *The Deer Hunter* and *Kramer vs Kramer*

11 ABBA, Santana, Simon and Garfunkel, The Rolling Stones, Bob Marley and the Wailers, Jean-Michel Jarre, Black Sabbath, Julio Iglesias, Fleetwood Mac, Stevie Wonder, Kraftwerk and Pink Floyd

---

Geography II

1 Niagara Falls

2 Bolivia and Peru

3 Greenland, New Guinea and Borneo

4 French, German, Italian and Romansh

5 The equator, the Arctic Circle, the Antarctic Circle, the Tropic of Cancer and the Tropic of Capricorn

6 Sahara, Arabian Desert, Gobi Desert, Kalahari Desert, Great Victoria Desert and Patagonian Desert

7 Africa, Asia, North America, South America, Antarctica, Australia and Europe

8 Italy, Australia, Chile, Northern Ireland, USA, Austria, Senegal and China

9 Mandarin Chinese, Spanish, English, Hindi, Arabic, Portuguese, Bengali, Russian and Japanese

10 Russia, Canada, USA, China, Brazil, Australia, India, Argentina, Kazakhstan and Algeria

11 African plate, Antarctic plate, Arabian plate, Australian plate, Caribbean plate, Cocos plate, Eurasian plate, Indian plate, Juan de Fuca plate, Nazca plate, North American plate, Pacific plate, Philippine plate, Scotia plate and South American plate

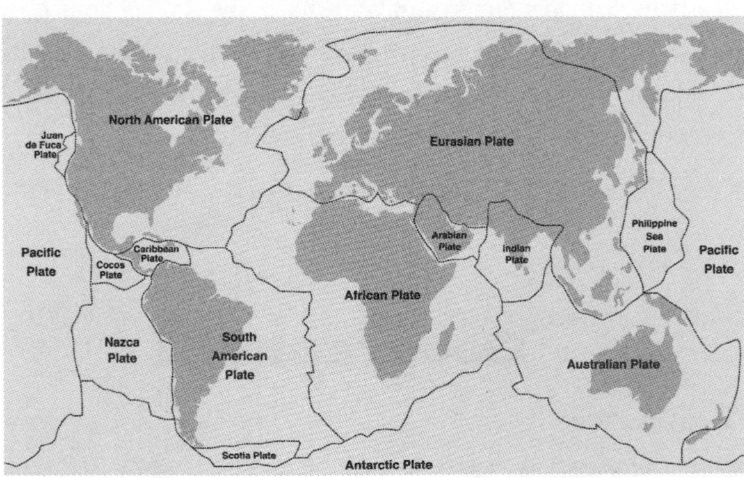

The Human Body

1 William Harvey

2 The windpipe and voicebox

3 The incus (or anvil), the malleus (or hammer) and the stapes (or stirrup)

4 Canines, incisors, molars and premolars

5 Hearing, sight, smell, taste and touch

6 Ball-and-socket, condyloid, gliding, hinge, pivot and saddle

7 Heart disease, stroke, lower respiratory infections, chronic obstructive pulmonary disease, cancers of the lung, trachea and bronchus, diabetes, and dementia

8 Brain, buttocks, jaw, foot, thigh, wrist, ankle, kidneys

9 Skin, liver, brain, lungs, heart, kidneys, spleen, pancreas and thyroid

10 Femur (thighbone), tibia (shinbone), fibula (lower leg), humerus (upper arm), ulna (inner lower arm), radius (outer lower arm), seventh rib, eighth rib, innominate bone (hipbone) and sternum (breastbone)

11 Aqueous humour, choroid, conjunctiva, cornea, iris, lens, optic nerve, pupil, retina, sclera, tear glands and vitreous humour

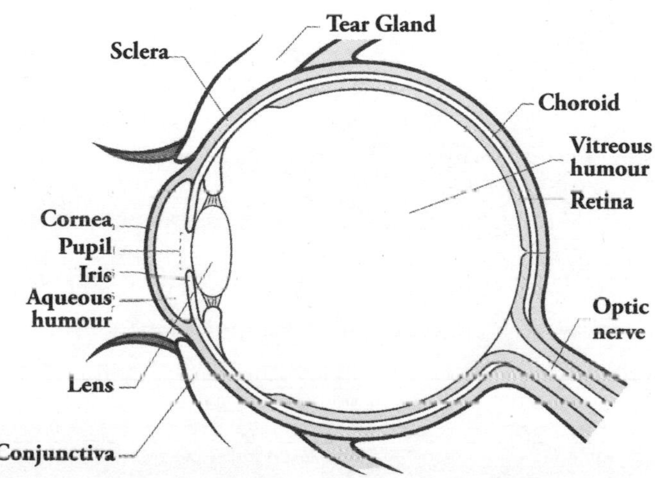

Religion

1 Voodoo

2 Cain and Abel

3 Rosh Hashanah, Yom Kippur and Hanukkah

4 Dukkha (the truth of suffering), Samudaya (the truth of the origin of suffering), Nirodha (the truth of the end of suffering) and Magga (the truth of the path that leads to the end of suffering)

5 Shahadah (testimony of faith), Salat or salah (prayer), Zakat (alms), Sawm (fasting during the month of Ramadan), Hajj (pilgrimage to Mecca)

6 John XXIII, Paul VI, John Paul I, John Paul II, Benedict XVI and Francis

7 Lust, gluttony, avarice, sloth, wrath, envy and pride

8 Brahma, Vishnu, Shiva, Krishna, Lakshmi, Durga, Ganesha and Hanuman

9 Confucianism, Hinduism, Buddhism, Judaism, Sikhism, Taoism, Zoroastrianism, Wicca and Shintoism

10 Water to blood, frogs, lice (or gnats), flies, livestock pestilence, boils, hail, locusts, darkness and death of the firstborn

11 Asher, Benjamin, Dan, Gad, Issachar, Joseph, Judah, Levi, Naphtali, Reuben, Simeon and Zebulun

---

Musicals I

1 *Oliver!*

2 Glinda the Good and Elphaba, the Wicked Witch of the West

3 Liza Minnelli, Michael York and Joel Grey

4 Frenchy, Jan, Marty and Rizzo

5 Roxie Hart, Velma Kelly, Billy Flynn, 'Mama' Morton and Mary Sunshine

6 *Cricket*, *Evita*, *Jesus Christ Superstar*, *Joseph and the Amazing Technicolor Dreamcoat*, *The Likes of Us* and *The Wizard of Oz*

7 Liesl, Friedrich, Louisa, Kurt, Brigitta, Marta and Gretl

8 Green Day, Frankie Valli and the Four Seasons, ABBA, Billy Joel, The Kinks, The Proclaimers, The Spice Girls and Queen

9 *Evita*, *Wicked*, *The King and I*, *My Fair Lady*, *Annie*, *Guys and Dolls*, *Oklahoma!*, *A Little Night Music* and *Carousel*

10 *Carousel*, *State Fair*, *Allegro*, *South Pacific*, *The King and I*, *Me and Juliet*, *Pipe Dream*, *Cinderella*, *Flower Drum Song and The Sound of Music*

11 *Saturday Night*, *West Side Story*, *Gypsy*, *A Funny Thing Happened on the Way to the Forum*, *Anyone Can Whistle*, *Do I Hear a Waltz?*, *Company*, *Follies*, *A Little Night Music*, *The Frogs*, *Pacific Overtures*, *Sweeney Todd*, *Merrily We Roll Along*, *Sunday in the Park with George*, *Into the Woods*, *Assassins*, *Passion* and *Bounce*

Life at Sea

1 The kraken

2 Port and starboard

3 Cleo, Marlin and Flounder

4 Bartolomeu Dias, Harold Holt, Robert Maxwell and Natalie Wood

5 Arctic, Atlantic, Indian, Pacific and Southern (Antarctic) (see opposite)

6 Black marlin, sailfish, striped marlin, wahoo, mako shark, Atlantic bluefin tuna

7 Whale shark, basking shark, great white shark, tiger shark, Pacific sleeper shark, Greenland shark and great hammerhead shark

8 Canada, Norway, Indonesia, Greenland, Russia, the Philippines, Japan and Australia

9 Challenger Deep (part of the Mariana Trench), Tonga Trench, Galathea Depth (part of the Philippine Trench), Kuril-Kamchatka Trench, Kermadec Trench, Izu-Ogasawara Trench, Japan Trench, Puerto Rico Trench and Yap Trench

10 Blue whale, fin whale, sperm whale, bowhead whale, right whale, humpback whale, grey whale, sei whale, Bryde's whale and Baird's beaked whale

11 *Pequod*, *Jolly Roger*, USS *Constitution*, *Rainbow Warrior*, HMS *Victory*, *Bismarck*, *Argo*, *Hispaniola*, RMS *Lusitania*, *Dawn Treader*, *Nautilus* and *Demeter*

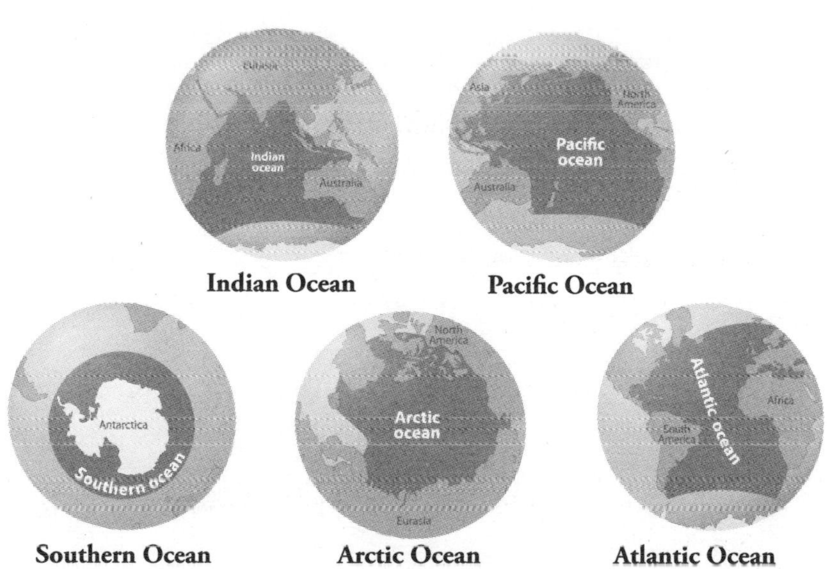

◀ (See opposite page) 5: The five oceans

General Knowledge IV

1 Rennet

2 Romulus and Remus

3 Chocolate, strawberry and vanilla

4 Australia, New Zealand, Switzerland and UK

5 Ant-Man, the Hulk, Iron Man, Thor and the Wasp

6 Arts & Literature, Entertainment, Geography, History, Science & Nature, and Sports & Leisure

7 Kilimanjaro, Everest, Mount McKinley, Aconcagua, Vinson Massif, Mount Kosciusko and Elbrus

8 Dr Dre, Pitbull, Snoop Dogg, Notorious BIG, 50 Cent, Eminem, Jay Z and Ice T

9 2, 3, 5, 7 11, 13, 17, 19 and 23

10 I am the Lord your God, You shall have no other gods before me; You shall not make any graven images of God; You shall not use the Lord your God's Name in vain; Remember the Sabbath day, to keep it Holy; Honour your father and mother; You shall not kill; You shall not commit adultery; You shall not steal; You shall not bear false witness against your neighbour; You shall not covet your neighbour's goods

11 Heights, flying, open spaces, spiders, clowns, women, mice, snakes, ghosts, fear, sleep and needles

The 1980s

1 Luigi

2 Ferdinand and Imelda Marcos

3 Moscow, Los Angeles and Seoul

4 Lech Wałęsa, Yuri Andropov, Corazon Aquino and Mikhail Gorbachev

5 Axl Rose, Duff McKagan, Izzy Stradlin, Slash and Steven Adler

6 Iran, West Germany, Egypt, South Africa, Israel and the Soviet Union

7 1981, 1989, 1986, 1984, 1983, 1980 and 1986

8 Joan Miró, Alfred Hitchcock, Ingrid Bergman, Thelonious Monk, Indira Gandhi, Anwar Sadat, Richard Feynman and Dian Fossey

9 Haruki Murakami, Marguerite Duras, Margaret Atwood, Salman Rushdie, Umberto Eco, Patrick Süskind, Kazuo Ishiguro, Milan Kundera and Isabel Allende

10 *Ordinary People*, *Chariots of Fire*, *Gandhi*, *Terms of Endearment*, *Amadeus*, *Out of Africa*, *Platoon*, *The Last Emperor*, *Rain Man* and *Driving Miss Daisy*

11 Bruce Springsteen, Dire Straits, Pixies, Paul Simon, Roxette, A-ha, Def Leppard, Youssou N'Dour, Phil Collins, Prince and The Revolution, Neneh Cherry and Madonna

---

Literature II

1 *A Suitable Boy*

2 Scarlett O'Hara and Rhett Butler

3 Athos, Porthos and Aramis

4 Meg, Jo, Beth and Amy

5 Anne, Dick, George, Julian and Timmy

6 Sam Spade, Inspector Morse, William Baskerville, Philip Marlowe, Kurt Wallander and C. Auguste Dupin

7 *A Game of Thrones*, *A Clash of Kings*, *A Storm of Swords*, *A Feast for Crows*, *A Dance with Dragons*, *The Winds of Winter* and *A Dream of Spring*

8 Lewis Carroll, Hergé, Joseph Conrad, Anne Rice, E. L. James, George Orwell, George Eliot and Dr Seuss

9 British Library, Library of Congress, Library and Archives Canada, New York Public Library, Russian State Library, Bibliothèque Nationale de France, National Library of Russia, National Diet Library (Japan) and the National Library of China

10 Anthony Burgess, Ian McEwan, Truman Capote (below), Alice Walker, Boris Pasternak, Michael Ondaatje, Mario Puzo, Ken Kesey and Thomas Harris

11 *Childhood, Boyhood, Youth, The Cossacks, War and Peace, Anna Karenina, Resurrection, Family Happiness, The Death of Ivan Ilyich, The Kreutzer Sonata, The Devil, The Forged Coupon* and *Hadji Murat*

North America

1 Honduras

2 Ben Johnson and Carl Lewis

3 Life, liberty and the pursuit of happiness

4 Mexico City, Ecatepec, Guadalajara, and Puebla

5 Superior, Michigan, Huron, Erie and Ontario

6 Barbados, the Bahamas, Trinidad and Tobago, Dominica, Dominican Republic, and Antigua and Barbuda

7 Calgary Flames, Edmonton Oilers, Montreal Canadiens, Ottawa Senators, Toronto Maple Leafs, Vancouver Canucks and the Winnipeg Jets

8 Brown University, Columbia University, Cornell University, Dartmouth College, Harvard University, the University of Pennsylvania, Princeton University and Yale University

9 New York City, Los Angeles, Chicago, Houston, Phoenix, Philadelphia, San Antonio, San Diego and Dallas

10 Alberta, British Columbia, Manitoba, New Brunswick, Newfoundland and Labrador, Nova Scotia, Ontario, Prince Edward Island, Quebec and Saskatchewan

11 Connecticut, Delaware, Georgia, Maryland, Massachusetts, New Hampshire, New Jersey, New York, North Carolina, Pennsylvania, Rhode Island, South Carolina and Virginia
(see map opposite)

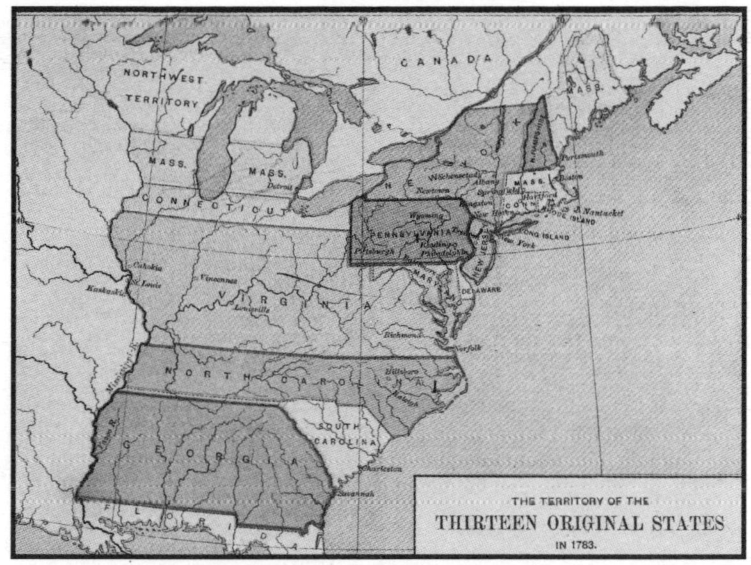

◀ (See opposite page) 11: The original thirteen US states

Mythology

1 Maya

2 *The Iliad* and *The Odyssey*

3 Ra, Isis and Anubis

4 Jupiter, Vesta, Venus and Mercury

5 *The Lightning Thief*, *The Sea of Monsters*, *The Titan's Curse*, *The Battle of the Labyrinth* and *The Last Olympian*

6 Two Travellers, Tortoise, Doves, Dolphin, Innkeeper, Sheep's Clothing

7 Harpy, Griffin, Centaur, Satyr, Mermaid, Unicorn and Pegasus

8 Cao Guojiu, Han Xiangzi, He Xian'gu, Lan Caihe, Li Tieguai, Lü Dongbin, Zhang Guolao and Zhongli Quan

9 Alfheim, Asgard, Helheim, Jotunheim, Midgard, Muspellheim, Niflheim, Svartalfheim and Vanaheim

10 Poseidon, Hades, Ares, Apollo, Hephaestus, Dionysus, Hypnos, Athena, Aphrodite and Artemis

11 Rat, ox, tiger, rabbit, dragon, snake, horse, goat, monkey, rooster, dog and pig

Plants and Trees

1 Tulip

2 Annuals and perennials

3 The Hundred Acre Wood, Sherwood Forest and Endor

4 Stamen, pistil, petals and stem

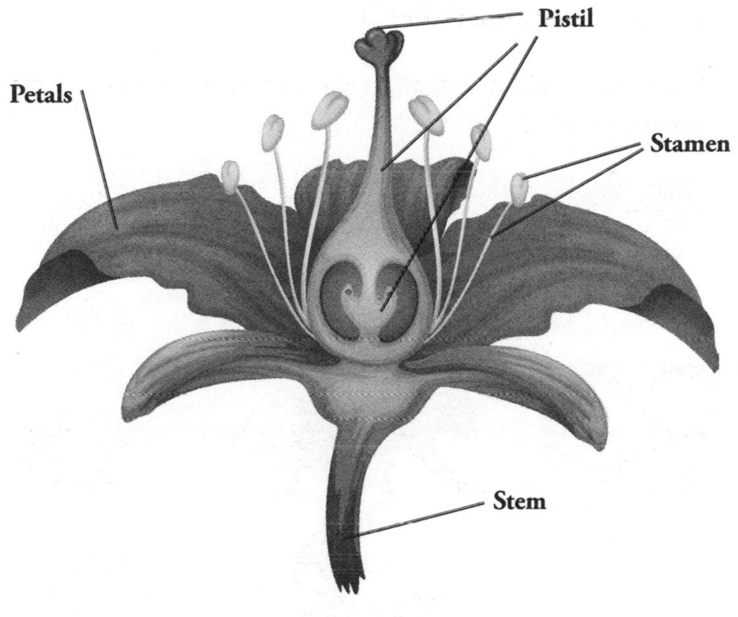

5 Dahlia, Daisy, Lotus, Rose and Lilacs

6 Bodhi Tree, chestnut, giant sequoia, cherry tree, apple tree and thorn

7 Maple, birch, chestnut, ash, poplar, pine and oak

8 Russia, Canada, Brazil, USA, China, Australia, Democratic Republic of the Congo and Argentina

9 Raspberry, blackcurrant, orange, pear, almond, lemon, hazelnut, cherry and melon

10 Snapdragon, cornflower, carnation, foxglove, sunflower, Busy Lizzie, sweet pea, lilac, snowdrop and baby's breath

11 Beijing, Florence, New York City, Mexico City, Stockholm, Munich, London, Paris, Perth, Bangkok, Osaka, Barcelona, São Paulo, Dublin, Vancouver and Tokyo

Space

1 Comets

2 Phobos and Deimos

3 Neil Armstrong, Buzz Aldrin and Michael Collins

4 Head, nucleus, coma, tails (ion and dust)

5 NASA (USA), CSA (Canada), ESA (Europe), JAXA (Japan) and Roscosmos (Russia)

6 Atlantis, Endeavour, Discovery, Challenger, Columbia and Enterprise

7 Nitrogen, oxygen, argon, carbon dioxide, neon, helium and methane

8 Mercury, Venus, Earth, Mars, Jupiter, Saturn, Uranus and Neptune

9 Jean-Luc Picard, William T. Riker, Data, Geordi La Forge, Worf, Beverly Crusher, Deanna Troi, Tasha Yar and Wesley Crusher

10 Pete Conrad, Alan Bean, Alan Shepard, Edgar Mitchell, David Scott, James Irwin, John Young, Charles Duke, Eugene Cernan and Harrison Schmitt

11 Aries, Taurus, Gemini, Cancer, Leo, Virgo, Libra, Scorpio, Sagittarius, Capricorn, Aquarius and Pisces

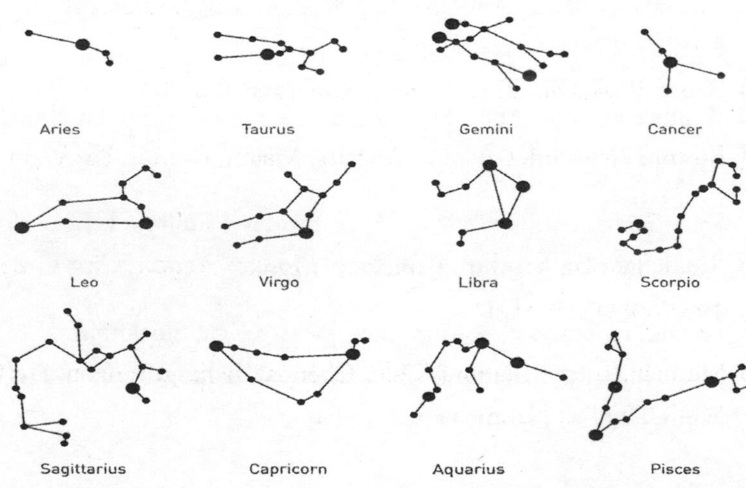

Cities

1 Mali

2 Reykjavik and Wellington

3 St Petersburg, Belize City and Lagos

4 Belfast, Cardiff, Edinburgh and London

5 The Bronx, Brooklyn, Manhattan, Queens and Staten Island

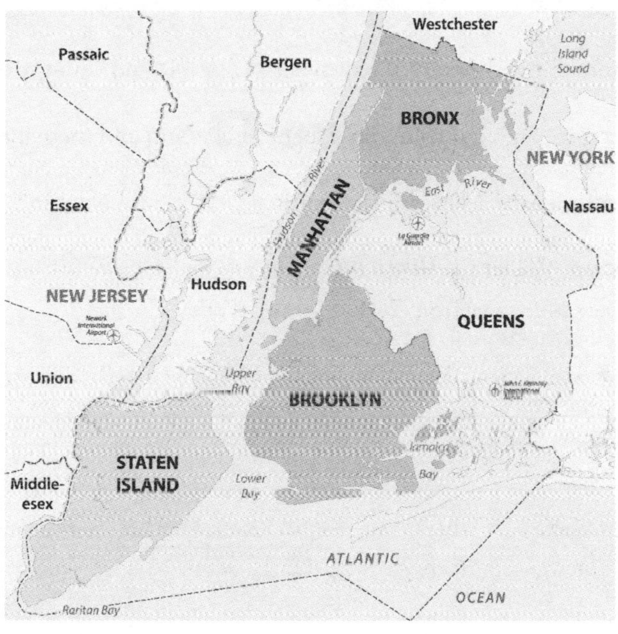

6 Rabat, Reykjavik, Riga, Riyadh, Rome and Roseau

7 Boston, New York City, Los Angeles, Miami, Detroit, Las Vegas and Chicago

8 Rio de Janeiro, Istanbul, Barcelona, Moscow, Vatican City, Cape Town, Agra and Xian

9 Mumbai, Tokyo, Istanbul, Oslo, Chennai, Beijing, Yangon, Ho Chi Minh City and Harare

10 River Molonglo, Río de la Plata, River Vltava, River Nile, River Seine, River Tigris, River Tiber, River Amstel, the Liffey and the Potomac River

11 Nigeria, Ethiopia, Lebanon, Senegal, Botswana, Zimbabwe, Indonesia, Jamaica, Peru, Belarus, Cyprus, Haiti, Ecuador, South Korea, Estonia and Namibia

---

Science II

1 Francis Bacon

2 Isaac Newton and Gottfried Wilhelm Leibniz

3 Protons, neutrons and electrons

4 Adenine, cytosine, guanine and thymine

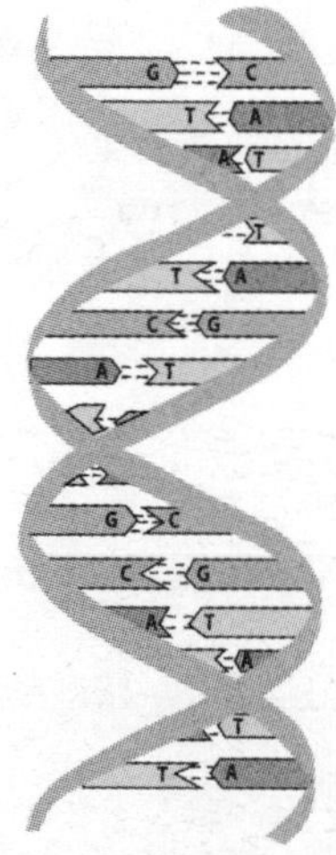

5 Marie Curie and Pierre Curie (1903, Physics); Frédéric Joliot and Irène Joliot-Curie (1935, Chemistry); Carl Cori and Gerty Cori (1947, Physiology or Medicine); May-Britt Moser and Edvard Moser (2014, Physiology or Medicine); Sir William Henry Bragg and William Lawrence Bragg (1915, Physics)

6 Argon, helium, krypton, neon, radon and xenon

7 Andromeda, Draco, Aquila, Ursa Major, Pavo, Scutum and Monoceros

8 212°F, 98.6°F, 69.8°F and 32°F; 373.15K, 310K, 294.15K and 273.15K

9 Stephen Hawking, Andreas Vesalius, Nicolaus Copernicus, Galileo Galilei, Isaac Newton, Rachel Carson, Carl Sagan, Oliver Sacks and Charles Darwin

10 Niels Bohr (bohrium), Pierre and Marie Curie (curium), Albert Einstein (einsteinium), Enrico Fermi (fermium), Ernest Lawrence (lawrencium), Dmitri Mendeleev (mendelevium), Lise Meitner (meitnerium), Alfred Nobel (nobelium), Ernest Rutherford (rutherfordium) and Wilhelm Roentgen (roentgenium)

11 Bees, cells, insects, women's health, blood, butterflies and moths, the nervous system, cancer, bones, illness, sleep and poisons

---

The 1990s

1 Yitzhak Rabin

2 Barcelona and Atlanta

3 Kurt Cobain, Dave Grohl and Krist Novoselic

4 1997, 1994, 1999 and 1991

5 Naomi Campbell, Cindy Crawford, Linda Evangelista, Tatjana Patitz and Christy Turlington

6 Chandler Bing, Phoebe Buffay, Monica Geller, Ross Geller, Rachel Green and Joey Tribbiani

7 Mika Häkkinen, Damon Hill, Nigel Mansell, Alain Prost, Michael Schumacher, Ayrton Senna and Jacques Villeneuve

8 Edward Bunker, Steve Buscemi, Harvey Keitel, Michael Madsen, Chris Penn, Tim Roth, Quentin Tarantino and Lawrence Tierney

9 *The Firm*, *The Pelican Brief*, *The Client*, *The Chamber*, *The Rainmaker*, *The Runaway Jury*, *The Partner*, *The Street Lawyer* and *The Testament*

10 *Dances with Wolves*, *The Silence of the Lambs*, *Unforgiven*, *Schindler's List*, *Forrest Gump*, *Braveheart*, *The English Patient*, *Titanic*, *Shakespeare in Love* and *American Beauty*

11 U2, 2Pac Shakur, Andrea Bocelli, Radiohead, Red Hot Chili Peppers, Michael Jackson, Jeff Buckley, Alanis Morissette, Beck, R.E.M., Ace of Base, New Kids on the Block, Pearl Jam, Sheryl Crow and Aqua

---

Musicals II

1 *Fiddler on the Roof*

2 Max Bialystock and Leo Bloom

3 The Scarecrow, the Tin Man and the Cowardly Lion

4 Sky Masterson, Sister Sarah Brown, Nathan Detroit and Miss Adelaide

5 Jean Valjean, Inspector Javert, Fantine, Éponine and Gavroche

6 Centipedes, dragonflies, katydids, locusts, mosquitos and moths

7 Adam, Benjamin, Caleb, Daniel, Ephraim, Frank and Gideon Pontipee

8 Gus, Macavity, Skimbleshanks, Jennyanydots, Grizabella, Bustopher Jones, Growltiger and Mr Mistoffelees

9 *The Phantom of the Opera*, *Chicago*, *The Lion King*, *Cats*, *Les Misérables*, *A Chorus Line*, *Oh! Calcutta!*, *Wicked* and *Mamma Mia!*

10 *The Broadway Melody*, *The Great Ziegfeld*, *Going My Way*, *An American in Paris*, *Gigi*, *West Side Story*, *My Fair Lady*, *The Sound of Music*, *Oliver!* and *Chicago*

11 Raindrops on roses, whiskers on kittens, bright copper kettles, warm woollen mittens, brown paper packages tied up with strings, cream coloured ponies, crisp apple strudels, doorbells, sleigh bells, schnitzel with noodles, wild geese that fly with the moon on their wings, girls in white dresses with blue satin sashes, snowflakes that stay on my nose and eyelashes, and silver white winters that melt into springs

---

Food and Drink II

1 Saffron

2 Eggs and ham

3 Bacon, lettuce and tomato

4 Michel and Albert, Alain (Michel's son) and Michel Jr (Albert's son)

5 Bitter, salty, sour, sweet and umami

6 Anton Chekov, Joanne Harris, Roald Dahl, Anthony Burgess, John Steinbeck and Fannie Flagg

7 Magnum, Jeroboam, Rehoboam, Methuselah, Salmanazar, Balthazar and Nebuchadnezzar

8 Mexico, Greece, Netherlands, Switzerland, Spain, USA, Italy and UK

9 Tagliatelle, pappardelle, rigatoni, spaghetti, linguine, stringozzi, fettuccine, fusilli and vermicelli

◄ (See opposite page) 9: Types of pasta

10 Japan, Poland, France, Australia, Germany, India, Italy, China, Russia and Mexico

11 Switzerland, South Africa, Czech Republic, USA, Iceland, France, Georgia, India, Italy, China, Greece, Portugal, Japan, Spain, Hungary and Mexico

Cinema III

1 Guillermo del Toro

2 Rick and Ilsa

3 *Pather Panchali*, *Aparajito* and *The World of Apu*

4 *Joe Versus the Volcano*, *Sleepless in Seattle*, *You've Got Mail* and *Ithaca*

5 *The Curse of the Black Pearl*, *Dead Man's Chest*, *At World's End*, *On Stranger Tides* and *Dead Men Tell No Tales*

6 *Alien*, *Aliens*, *Alien 3*, *Alien Resurrection*, *Prometheus* and *Alien: Covenant*

7 *Spirited Away*, *Howl's Moving Castle*, *Ponyo*, *Princess Mononoke*, *The Secret World of Arrietty*, *The Wind Rises* and *Tales from Earthsea*

8 Stanley Kubrick, Martin Scorsese, Federico Fellini, David Lynch, Sergio Leone, John Huston, Clint Eastwood and Sam Peckinpah

9 *The Silence of the Lambs*, *This is Spinal Tap*, *Chicken Run*, *Back to the Future*, *Cool Runnings*, *Ferris Bueller's Day Off*, *Men in Black*, *The Matrix* and *King Kong*

10 *ET the Extra-Terrestrial*, *The Color Purple*, *Schindler's List*, *Saving Private Ryan*, *Munich*, *Letters from Iwo Jima*, *War Horse*, *Lincoln*, *Bridge of Spies* and *The Post*

11 *Star Trek: The Motion Picture*, *Star Trek II: The Wrath of Khan*, *Star Trek III: The Search for Spock*, *Star Trek IV: The Voyage Home*, *Star Trek V: The Final Frontier*, *Star Trek VI: The Undiscovered Country*, *Star Trek Generations*, *Star Trek: First Contact*, *Star Trek: Insurrection*, *Star Trek: Nemesis*, *Star Trek*, *Star Trek Into Darkness* and *Star Trek Beyond*

General Knowledge V

1 Chess

2 Laurel and Hardy

3 Alvin, Simon and Theodore

4 Black, cyan, magenta and yellow

5 Anna Pavlova (pavlova), Margherita of Savoy (margherita), Dame Nelly Melba (peach Melba), John Montagu, 4th Earl of Sandwich (the sandwich), Giuseppe Garibaldi (Garibaldi biscuit)

6 Adam West, Michael Keaton, Val Kilmer, George Clooney, Christian Bale and Ben Affleck

7 George Washington, Thomas Jefferson, Abraham Lincoln, Alexander Hamilton, Andrew Jackson, Ulysses S. Grant and Benjamin Franklin

8 *Agnes Grey*, *Jane Eyre*, *Shirley*, *The Green Dwarf*, *The Professor*, *The Tenant of Wildfell Hall*, *Villette* and *Wuthering Heights*

9 China, France, India, Israel, North Korea, Pakistan, Russia, UK and USA

10 Jack Brabham, Juan Manuel Fangio, Lewis Hamilton, Niki Lauda, Nelson Piquet, Alain Prost, Ayrton Senna, Michael Schumacher, Jackie Stewart and Sebastian Vettel

11 Garnet, amethyst, bloodstone, sapphire, agate, emerald, onyx, carnelian, peridot/chrysolite, beryl, topaz and ruby

---

The Arts II

1 Walter Sickert

2 Donatello and Auguste Rodin

3 Caravaggio, El Greco and Tintoretto

4 Louis Réard, Levi Strauss, Coco Chanel and Mary Quant

5 Auguste Rodin, Pablo Picasso, Andy Warhol, Gustav Klimt and Jeff Koons

6 Impressionism, the Baroque, the Pre-Raphaelite Brotherhood, Surrealism, Pop Art and Bauhaus

7 Samba, waltz, disco, cha-cha, Charleston, Argentine tango and breakdancing

8 San Diego, Milan, New York City, Bayreuth, Paris, Buenos Aires, Moscow and London

9 A bending of the knee or knees; a jump from one foot to the other in which the working leg is brushed into the air; a position on one leg with the other raised behind the body and extended; a turn in the air; lifting off the floor on one leg, and landing on two; positioning the feet and legs out from the hip joints to a ninety-degree position; rotation of the body on one foot; standing with legs crossed at an angle to the audience; the same as the last position but with the knee of the extended leg bent.

10 *Norma*, *La Bohème*, *Carmen*, *Rigoletto*, *The Barber of Seville*, *Turandot*, *Carmina Burana*, *Gianni Schicchi*, *Eugene Onegin* and *The Magic Flute*

11 Pieter Bruegel, Diego Velázquez, Pierre-Auguste Renoir, Peter Paul Rubens, Canaletto, Paul Cézanne, Edgar Degas, Diego Rivera, Salvador Dalí, Edvard Munch, Claude Monet and Wassily Kandinsky

Oceania

1 Ayers Rock

2 Auckland and Christchurch

3 The wallaby, the palm and the silver fern

4 Hawaii, Maui, O'ahu and Kaua'i

5 Murray River, Murrumbidgee River, Darling River, Lachlan River and Warrego River

6 AC/DC, Kylie Minogue, INXS, Nick Cave and the Bad Seeds, Olivia Newton-John and Crowded House

7 Auckland, Dunedin, Brisbane, Melbourne, Sydney, Perth and Wellington

8 Adelaide, Brisbane, Canberra, Darwin, Hobart, Melbourne, Perth and Sydney

9 Tim Winton, Marcus Clarke, Ruth Park, Miles Franklin, Peter Carey, Joan Lindsay, Bryce Courtenay, Christos Tsiolkas and Jeannie (Mrs Aeneas) Gunn

10 Fiji, Kiribati, Micronesia, Palau, Papua New Guinea, Samoa, the Solomon Islands, Tonga, Tuvalu and Vanuatu

11 Sir Robert Menzies, Harold Holt, John McEwen, John Gorton, William McMahon, Gough Whitlam, Malcolm Fraser, Bob Hawke, Paul Keating, John Howard, Kevin Rudd, Julia Gillard, Tony Abbott and Malcolm Turnbull

---

History II

1 Charlemagne

2 France and UK

3 Wilhelm I, Frederick III and Wilhelm II

4 Galba, Otho, Vitellius and Vespasian

5 Fidel Castro, Sun Yat-sen, Maximilien de Robespierre, Ahmed Ben Bella and Simón Bolívar

6 Morocco, Monaco, the Netherlands, Saudi Arabia, Tonga and Bhutan

7 Joan of Arc, Hannibal, Alexander the Great, Erwin Rommel, Gustavus Adolphus, Suleiman the Magnificent and Genghis Khan

8 Archduke Franz Ferdinand, Martin Luther King Jr, Spencer Perceval, John F. Kennedy, William McKinley, Anna Lindh, Mahatma Gandhi and Rajiv Gandhi

9 Konrad Adenauer, Ludwig Erhard, Kurt Georg Kiesinger, Willy Brandt, Walter Scheel, Helmut Schmidt, Helmut Kohl, Gerhard Schröder and Angela Merkel

10 1648 treaty that ended the Thirty Years' War and the Eighty Years' War; 1713 treaty that ended War of the Spanish Succession; 1842 treaty that ended First Opium War; 1895 treaty that ended the First Sino-Japanese War; 1898 treaty that ended the Spanish-American War; 1905 treaty that ended the Russo-Japanese War; 1918 treaty between Soviet Russia and Germany; 1919 treaty agreed at the end of the First World War; 1978 agreement largely normalizing relations between Anwar Sadat's Egypt and Menachem Begin's Israel; 1998 agreement that paved way for devolved government in Northern Ireland

11 1865, 1815, 1936, 570, 1986, 312, 1649, 1793, 753 BC, 1941, 49 BC and 1917

The 2000s

1 Guantanamo Bay

2 Mike Myers and Cameron Diaz

3 Sydney, Athens and Beijing

4 *Twilight, New Moon, Eclipse* and *Breaking Dawn*

5 Rudy Giuliani, George W. Bush, You, Vladimir Putin and Ben Bernanke

6 Afghanistan, China, Brazil, Pakistan, Italy and the Czech Republic

7 2007, 2008, 2009, 2004, 2003, 2005 and 2001

8 Leni Riefenstahl, Billy Wilder, Victor Borge, Arthur Miller, Walter Cronkite, Evel Knievel, Stieg Larsson, Steve Irwin

9 Roberto Bolaño, Ian McEwan, David Mitchell, Yann Martel, Orhan Pamuk, Junot Diaz, Jonathan Franzen, Khaled Hosseini, Cormac McCarthy and Hilary Mantel

10 *Gladiator*, *A Beautiful Mind*, *Chicago*, *The Lord of the Rings: The Return of the King*, *Million Dollar Baby*, *Crash*, *The Departed*, *No Country for Old Men*, *Slumdog Millionaire* and *The Hurt Locker*

11 Kings of Leon, Green Day, Amy Winehouse, Jay-Z, The White Stripes, Arcade Fire, Kanye West, The Strokes, M.I.A., Radiohead, Coldplay and Arctic Monkeys

---

Sport II

1 Sumo wrestling

2 Steffi Graf and Angelique Kerber

3 Japan, the Netherlands and Spain

4 The Australian Open, French Open, US Open and Wimbledon

5 Point guard, shooting guard, centre, small forward and power forward

6 Touchdown, extra point, two-point conversion, field goal, safety and fair catch kick

7 100m hurdles, high jump, shot put, 200m, long jump, javelin and 800m

8 Heavyweight, cruiserweight (junior heavyweight), middleweight, welterweight, lightweight, featherweight, bantamweight and flyweight

9 The New York Yankees (formerly New York Highlanders/ Baltimore Orioles), St Louis Cardinals, Oakland Athletics (formerly Philadelphia/Kansas City), San Francisco Giants (formerly New York), Boston Red Sox (formerly Boston Americans), Los Angeles Dodgers (formerly Brooklyn), Cincinnati Reds (formerly Redlegs and Red Stockings), Pittsburgh Pirates and Detroit Tigers

10 Tiger Woods, Greg Norman, Nick Faldo, Rory McIlroy, Seve Ballesteros, Luke Donald, Jason Day, Dustin Johnson, Ian Woosnam and Nick Price

11 Ajax, Barcelona, Bayern Munich, Benfica, Inter Milan (Internazionale), Juventus, Liverpool, Manchester United, AC Milan, Nottingham Forest, Porto and Real Madrid

---

Monsters in Fact and Fiction

1 Godzilla

2 O. C. Marsh and Edward Drinker Cope

3 Saltwater, Nile and Orinoco

4 Green anaconda, Burmese python, Reticulated python and African rock python

5 *Jurassic Park*, *The Lost World: Jurassic Park*, *Jurassic Park III*, *Jurassic World* and *Jurassic World: Fallen Kingdom*

6 Japan, USA, UK, Sweden, Mexico, Australia and South Korea

7 Mosquitoes, tsetse flies, snakes, scorpions, hippopotami, crocodiles and elephants

8 *Child's Play*, *A Nightmare on Elm Street*, *Scream*, *Silence of the Lambs*, *Friday 13th*, *The Texas Chainsaw Massacre*, *Halloween* and *Hellraiser*

9 Yeti, the Sphinx, Sasquatch or Bigfoot, the Chimera, Golem, Thyphon, Banshee, Medusa and Lernaean Hydra

10 Bram Stoker, H. P. Lovecraft, Mary Shelley, Julia Donaldson, Arthur Conan Doyle, Lewis Carroll, J. K. Rowling, Robert Louis Stevenson, Stephen King and Homer

11 Diplodocus, oviraptor, triceratops, ichthyosaurus, megatherium, smilodon, stegosaurus, velociraptor, deinonychus, Tyrannosaurus rex, euoplocephalus and pterodactyl

Literature III

1 Aeschylus

2 Jem and Scout

3 Inferno, Purgatorio and Paradiso

4 *My Brilliant Friend*, *The Story of a New Name*, *Those Who Leave and Those Who Stay* and *The Story of the Lost Child*

5 *Angels & Demons*, *The Da Vinci Code*, *The Lost Symbol*, *Inferno* and *Origin*

6 *Sense and Sensibility*, *Pride and Prejudice*, *Mansfield Park*, *Emma*, *Persuasion* and *Northanger Abbey*

7 *The Name of the Rose*, *Foucault's Pendulum*, *The Island of the Day Before*, *Baudolino*, *The Mysterious Flame of Queen Loana*, *The Prague Cemetery* and *Numero Zero*

8 Voltaire, Immanuel Kant, Erasmus, Thomas Hobbes, Roland Barthes, Francis Bacon, Niccolò Machiavelli and Mary Wollstonecraft

9 Arryn, Baratheon, Greyjoy, Lannister, Martell, Stark, Targaryen, Tully and Tyrell

10 Graham Greene, Yukio Mishima, Jack Kerouac, E. M. Forster, Gustave Flaubert, Gregory David Roberts, Franz Kafka, Fyodor Doestoevsky, Manuel Puig and Evelyn Waugh

11 *Along Came a Spider*, *Kiss the Girls*, *Jack and Jill*, *Cat and Mouse*, *Pop Goes the Weasel*, *Roses Are Red*, *Violets Are Blue*, *Four Blind Mice*, *The Big Bad Wolf*, *London Bridges*, *Mary, Mary*, *Cross*, *Double Cross*

Famous People II

1 Napoléon Bonaparte

2 Nicholas Sarkozy and Carla Bruni

3 Beyoncé Knowles, Kelly Rowland and Michelle Williams

4 Jimmy Page, John Bonham, John Paul Jones and Robert Plant

5 Danny Wood, Donnie Wahlberg, Joey McIntyre, Jonathan Knight and Jordan Knight

6 Chris Evans, Robert Downey Jr, Chris Hemsworth, Mark Ruffalo, Scarlett Johansson and Jeremy Renner

7 Alan, Donny, Jay, 'Little' Jimmy, Marie, Merrill and Wayne

8 Abraham Lincoln, Martin Luther King, Julius Caesar, René Descartes, Isaac Newton, Thomas Edison, Socrates and Barack Obama

9 George Washington, John Adams, Thomas Jefferson, James Madison, James Monroe, John Quincy Adams, Andrew Jackson, Martin Van Buren and William Henry Harrison

10 Nelson Mandela, Oscar Wilde, Barack Obama, Maya Angelou, Adolf Hitler, Michael Jackson, Mahatma Gandhi, Karen Blixen, Robert Graves and Bill Gates

11 Peter (originally Simon), Andrew, James (the Greater), John, Philip, Bartholomew (or Nathaniel), Thomas, Matthew (or Levi), James the Less, Lebbaeus (or Thaddaeus or Jude), Simon the Zealot and Judas Iscariot

---

Music III

1 Paul Anka

2 Russia and Japan

3 Violins, pianos and guitars

4 Bill Berry, Peter Buck, Mike Mills and Michael Stipe

5 Cello, piano, violin, guitar and flute

6 Eminem, Madonna, Cher, Prince, Whitney Houston and Michael Jackson

7 Sandie Shaw, Dana, ABBA, Céline Dion, Dana International, Lordi and Conchita Wurst

8 The Eurythmics, The Go-Gos, Blondie, The Supremes, The Eagles, Wham!, Genesis and The Police

9 Henry Mancini, Lalo Schifrin, Ennio Morricone, Max Steiner, Elmer Bernstein, Hans Zimmer, Georges Delerue, John Williams and Michel Legrand

10 Coda, libretto, allegro, crescendo, diminuendo, fortissimo, a cappella, con amore, sotto and prima donna

11 Strings: violins (first and second), violas, cellos, double basses and harp; Woodwind: flutes, oboes, clarinets and bassoons; Brass: horns, trumpets, trombones and tuba; Percussion: timpani, bass drum, snare drum and cymbals

South America

1 The Pampas

2 Barcelona and Sevilla

3 Brazil, Colombia and Ecuador

4 Feijoada, empanada, chimichurri, picarones

5 Bolivia, Guyana, Paraguay, Suriname and Uruguay

6 Santiago, Bogotá, São Paulo, Lima, Buenos Aires and Caracas

7 Peru, Chile, Nicaragua, Bolivia, Venezuela, Argentina and Brazil

8 Brazil, Venezuela, Ecuador, Peru, Venezuela, Argentina, Uruguay and Bolivia

9 Mario Vargas Llosa, Carlos Fuentes, Jorge Luis Borges, Gabriel García Márquez, Paulo Coelho, Roberto Bolaño, Octavio Paz, Ernesto Che Guevara and Pablo Neruda

10 Friaça, Vavá, Pelé, Zagallo, Amarildo Tavares da Silveira, Zito, Gérson, Jairzinho, Carlos Alberto and Ronaldo

11 Buenos Aires, Sucre (*de jure*) and La Paz (*seat of government*), Brasilia, Santiago, Bogotá, Quito, Georgetown, Asunción, Lima, Paramaribo, Montevideo and Caracas

Technology and Innovation

1 The Falcon Heavy

2 Thomas Edison and George Westinghouse

3 James Hargreaves, Thomas Newcomen and Robert Stephenson

4 The Burj Khalifa (Dubai), the Shanghai Tower, the Makkah Royal Clock Tower (Mecca) and the Ping An Finance Center (Shenzhen)

5 Half-Life, Tomb Raider, The Legend of Zelda, Pokémon and Final Fantasy

6 Sellotape (or Scotch tape), Velcro, Tupperware, MacIntosh, Hoover and Jacuzzi

7 Nokia, Apple, Samsung, Motorola, HTC, Sony Ericsson and BlackBerry (formerly known as Research In Motion Limited/RIM)

8 Walter Gropius, Filippo Brunelleschi, Gian Lorenzo Bernini, Antoni Gaudí, Frank Lloyd Wright, Christopher Wren, Jørn Utzon and James Hoban

9 Lazlo Biro, Alfred Nobel, Clarence Birdseye, Frank Whittle, Percy Spencer, Gustaf Erik Pasch, René Laënnec, Alexander Graham Bell and Tim Berners-Lee

10 American Standard Code for Information Interchange, HyperText Markup Language, HyperText Transfer Protocol, Internet Service Provider, Portable Document Format, Text-to-Speech, Uniform Resource Locator, Universal Serial Bus, User experience, Central Processing Unit

11 Facebook, Amazon.com, Microsoft, Nintendo, Sony, Google Inc, eBay Inc, IBM (International Business Machines), Apple Inc, Samsung and Yahoo!

The 2010s

1 South Sudan

2 London and Rio de Janeiro

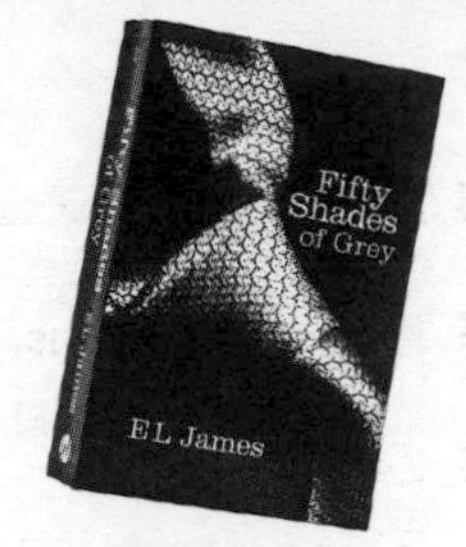

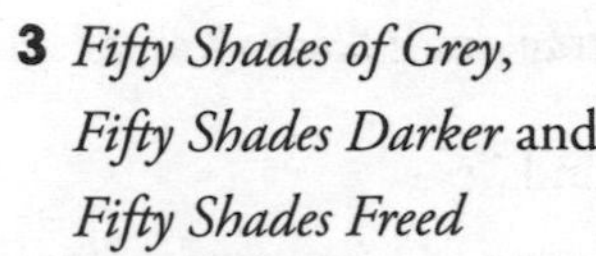

3 *Fifty Shades of Grey*, *Fifty Shades Darker* and *Fifty Shades Freed*

4 *Speak Now*, *Red*, *1989* and *Reputation*

5 Mark Zuckerberg, Barack Obama, Pope Francis, Angela Merkel and Donald Trump

6 Greece, Argentina, New Zealand, Canada, Venezuela and China

7 2017, 2015, 2010, 2011, 2013, 2012 and 2016

8 Nelson Mandela, Lucian Freud, Margaret Thatcher, Hugh Hefner, Ariel Sharon, Elie Wiesel, Wes Craven and Wangari Maathai

9 Anthony Doerr, John Green, Arundhati Roy, Gillian Flynn, Kate Atkinson, Herman Koch, Emma Donoghue, Julian Barnes and Jennifer Egan

10 Katy Perry, Justin Bieber, Barack Obama, Rihanna, Taylor Swift, Ellen DeGeneres, Lady Gaga, YouTube, Cristiano Ronaldo and Justin Timberlake

11 Adele, Lady Gaga, Lana Del Rey, Rihanna, Florence and the Machine, Lorde, Daft Punk, Mumford & Sons, Drake, Katy Perry, Bruno Mars and One Direction

---

General Knowledge VI

1 Golf

2 Snoopy and Woodstock

3 Hop, skip and jump

4 Harold Ramis, Rick Moranis, Bill Murray and Dan Aykroyd

5 Acheron, Cocytus, Phlegethon, Lethe and Styx

6 California (Disneyland), Florida (Walt Disney World), Tokyo (Disney Resort), Paris (Disneyland), Hong Kong (Disneyland Resort) and Shanghai (Disney Resort)

7 Aventine, Caelian, Capitoline, Esquiline, Palatine, Quirinal and Viminal

8 The European Free Trade Association; Food and Agriculture Organization; International Atomic Energy Agency; International Committee of the Red Cross; Organization of Petroleum Exporting Countries; United Nations Educational, Scientific and Cultural Organization; World Health Organization; World Intellectual Property Organization

9 Solitude, books and reading, dancing, money, alcohol, stealing, a single object or idea, fire or starting fires, and stamps

10 Bolivia, Ecuador, Colombia, Ethiopia, Bhutan, Eritrea, Yemen, Mexico, Iran and Kenya

11 Russia, Greece, Ireland, Hong Kong, Bhutan, Israel, United Arab Emirates, Bahrain, Spain, the Netherlands, Germany and Estonia

Picture credits

Page 39: Clipart.com

Page 110: Moviestore Collection / REX / Shutterstock

Page 144: Till Niermann / CC BY-SA 3.0

Page 149, 185, 191: Library of Congress Prints and Photographs Division

Pages 58, 159, 170, 176, 205, 206 (right), 209 (top right): Public Domain

Page 161: Globe Photos Inc. / REX / Shutterstock

Page 179: Keystone Archives / HIP / TopFoto

Page 189: Sipa Press / REX / Shutterstock

Page 209 (top left): Wolfgang Sauber / CC BY-SA 3.0

Page 223: Renata3 / CC BY-SA 4.0

All other images from Shutterstock.com